Responsible
Managers
Get Results

Responsible Managers Get Results

How the Best Find Solutions—Not Excuses

Gerald W. Faust
Richard I. Lyles
Will Phillips

AMACOM
American Management Association

New York • Atlanta • Boston • Chicago • Kansas City • San Francisco • Washington, D.C.
Brussels • Mexico City • Tokyo • Toronto

Library of Congress Cataloging-in-Publication Data

Faust, Gerald W.
    Responsible managers get results : how the best find solutions—
not excuses / Gerald W. Faust, Richard I. Lyles, and Will Phillips.
        p.   cm.
    Includes bibliographical references and index.
    ISBN 0-8144-0389-1 (hardcover)
    1. Teams in the workplace.   2. Problem solving.   3. Management.
I. Lyles, Richard I.   II. Phillips, Will.   III. Title.
    HD66.F38   1998
    658.4'03—dc21   97-44089
                                                                CIP

Printing number

10   9   8   7   6   5   4   3   2   1

We dedicate this book to our wives, *Terrie, Martha,* and *Mary.* These women have supported us, encouraged us, and helped us in so many ways. They inspire us with their caring and wisdom, and they console us when things get difficult. They have put up with us for so many years that we continue to be amazed at how lucky we are to have them as partners.

Contents

Acknowledgments

Heartfelt thanks go to Amy Rico Faust, and all the staff at Faust Management Corporation.

We also thank our families, friends, and colleagues for their tremendous support and input throughout the project.

Special thanks go to Rick Barrera, who did a terrific job of proofreading, making editorial suggestions, and critiquing our content. He did so under tremendous time constraints and gave the best kind of help anyone could ask for on a project of this type.

There have been many thinkers, writers, and practitioners whose ideas have inspired and enlightened us. Among those we wish to give special recognition to are Ichak Adizes and Ken and Margie Blanchard. Adizes helped bring two of us together and was a colleague whose ideas stimulated our thinking and laid a base for understanding organizations and change. Ken Blanchard has been a friend and colleague who was always prepared both to learn and to teach.

Finally, we would like to thank our many clients who have worked with us to create responsible organizations. We have learned with them. We appreciate their trust, and we respect the vision and effort it has taken for them to manage and lead so responsibly. We consider them all friends, colleagues, and contributors to all we do.

Introduction

The management fads of recent years are being abandoned, the victims of a worldwide return to the fundamental philosophies that have always produced sustained, reliable results. What are these fundamental philosophies?

We have been engaged in an ongoing search for the answer to this question for several decades. An important lesson we learned early on is that the solutions to complex management challenges are not found in buzzwords. We also learned early on that some of the most widely accepted notions about what it takes to be successful in management are invalid.

Many events have aided our learning, but one experience that helped frame our thinking happened years ago. We were engaged in a lively conversation with a friend of ours who is a business broker. The conversation focused on a topic near and dear to us all—the reasons why businesses succeed or fail. As the conversation developed and grew more animated, the focus shifted from why *businesses* succeed and fail to why *businesspeople* succeed and fail. Before long, the conversation centered on a particular businessman who was extraordinarily successful, even though we would never have predicted that he would be so. He didn't seem to have many of the characteristics that most of us consider essential for success in the competitive world of business. Most of all, he just didn't seem to be very bright. Someone in the group observed, "If he can achieve that level of success with his brains, then we all ought to go into that business. We'd be millionaires in no time!"

In just a few seconds, however, the streetwise business broker framed the issue in a much more practical and realistic way by responding, "You're drawing the wrong conclusions from the data. If he can succeed at such a phenomenal level, and he isn't that bright, then maybe brainpower isn't the prerequisite for success. I'd encourage you to stay away from that business until you know for sure why he is successful."

He went on to say that he'd seen many very bright people take over perfectly viable businesses and run them into the ground. His conclusion was that brainpower alone is not a causal factor in achieving success. Our combined experience in managing our own businesses, and in our research and management consulting, over the last three decades validates that conclusion. Intelligence by itself will never guarantee success. This view, gleaned from our experiences in the business world, is supported by a number of recent books.[1]

If intelligence isn't enough, then what is? What will guarantee success in business or management? Is it leadership? Communication skills? The ability to plan, organize, staff, develop, and control? It's arguable that any of these is the one right answer; if one were, then all businesses today should be successful, because all these topics have been fully explored in books, cassettes, videotapes, and courses.

Certainly, communication, motivation, planning, leadership, and all the factors normally discussed under the headings of management and business administration are important. And at one time or another, all are important contributors to positive results. But we think another factor supersedes all these as the primary determinant of success in management. That factor is responsibility—being responsible enough to do what it takes to produce the necessary results and to do what it takes to achieve success with the hand one has been dealt.

The Importance of Responsibility

One client of ours gained a valuable insight early in his career, as a young naval officer fresh out of college aboard a destroyer. The ship was one of three sister ships that were identical, having been built in the same shipyard, from the same blueprints, at almost exactly the same time and commissioned into the same squadron within a six-month time period. Personnel were assigned to the ships from the same personnel pool, the ships went through the same training schedules, and they got all their supplies and repair parts through the same supply system. The only difference among the three ships over time was their performance.

One of the ships was forever breaking down, unable to meet its operating schedule, and scoring poorly on exercises. The ship was also dirty, the sailors' uniforms looked sloppy, and the shipboard climate was characterized by a total lack of pride. The second ship was just the opposite. It never experienced a serious breakdown, always scored excellently on exercises and inspections, and, perhaps most important, always met every operational commitment with a little extra to spare. The ship and the sailors always looked sharp and evidenced great pride. The third ship was in the middle, average at everything.

What made the difference? Our client concluded that the distinguishing characteristic was how the different officers and crews viewed responsibility for results. The top-performing ship was led by responsible managers; the others were not.

Over time all three ships faced the same equipment, people, and operational problems. The top performers accepted responsibility for producing the desired result no matter what the problem was. Those who achieved lesser levels of performance were too eager to let the responsibility fall elsewhere, giving excuses such as, "The generator keeps breaking down," or "We can't get the parts we need from the supply center."

Similar comparisons can be found in franchised industries. Every franchisor will tell you that one of the most remarkable aspects of their business is the inexplicable inconsistencies that exist among franchisees. How can two franchisees with such similar locations, operating systems, marketing programs, equipment, technology, and market positioning produce such dramatically different results?

The poor performers would be the first to blame it on location, some uniqueness in their particular store, or a peculiar attitude of the customers in their area. But in every franchise network of sufficient size, it is possible to find a store in a worse location that is performing better. It is also possible to find other stores with similar characteristics that are still substantially out-performing the problem stores. In other words, the excuses for poor performance can always be invalidated. At the same time, the top performers have found solutions to all the problems the poor performers are living with.

Very simply stated, successful managers are responsible managers. They focus on the results that need to be produced and do whatever is necessary to achieve them. In order to maintain this focus on results, it's important that they do two things: First, they must elevate the role of problem solving in their organizations; they must make problem solving a strategic process. Second, they must solve the day-to-day problems that arise in their organizations decisively and permanently.

If a manager can do all this, we're confident that he will be successful in both the short and the long term. As for the chief executive officer in an organization, his role is to get everyone in the organization to do these same things. Responsible organizations are successful organizations.

Why aren't all organizations responsible and successful? The answer comes in two parts. The first, discussed below, deals with our culture. The second deals with individual management attitudes and abilities. It is what this book is about.

Barriers to Responsibility

The barriers to responsibility exist in society at large as well as in the mind-sets of individuals. The problems in society start at the top. In the United States we have an executive branch of government within which spin control has become the most important priority. It's not what you do that is important—for instance, results that would lead to a healthy economy or improved standards of living for our citizens—it's what you can get people to say or think about what you do.

The legislative branch of the U.S. government has been no more responsible. The norm of members of Congress is to spend way beyond our means, initiate programs with no accountability for results, and blame everything and everyone else for their inability to make things better. Government at all levels in many other countries has mimicked the worst of U.S. government practices. Much of this shift to irresponsibility is epitomized by the emergence, starting in the 1960s, of the "me" generation and the demand for "entitlements," which has led to a surge in the growth of taxes.

Although people often criticize the "tax and spend" attitudes of their governments, few do much to change it. Instead, as a society, we catch the disease in a slightly different form. People begin to find ways to get what they feel they have coming; they develop strategies to get what they can without accepting the responsibility for any adverse consequences suffered by others or society as a whole. Many companies, led by people with this mind-set, behave in a similar manner. Finally, many industries, comprised of companies with leaders possessing this mind-set, also follow along.

The media have a stake in not putting too much stock in accountability. In fact, the media are at least as irresponsible as political leaders.

In short, the premise of "freedom without responsibility" has become a key philosophical underpinning of much public policy and hence of society's thinking. We now have an entire generation that has been acculturated to avoid responsibility. The individual corollary is "I don't have to worry about the consequences of not performing as long as I have something or someone to blame it on." So what we have is a generation of teachers who can't teach because the system isn't focused on the classroom, a generation of doctors who can't practice medicine because the guidelines established by providers are too restrictive, and so on down the line.

But of most concern to us are managers who can't manage properly because they've become conditioned not to accept responsibility. "We can't be as profitable as we'd like because of the economy." "We can't fulfill our obligations to the environment and the community because they cost too much." "We don't have time to take care of our people." And again, the list goes on.

As long as we can say that the shortcoming occurred through some fault other than our own, it has become generally accepted practice to produce shortfalls. If heads of government can do it, if legislatures can do it, if the medical profession can do it, then why shouldn't we all do it? After all, we're just ordinary people out to make a buck and maybe get ahead in the management profession.

Overcoming the Barriers

Responsible managers are different. Responsible managers care about results and aren't interested in excuses. They care about doing what's right and are not interested in justifying expenditures of energy or resources in activities that don't contribute to positive results. Responsible managers have the courage to stand up and be counted. They are committed to contribution-oriented performance and are willing to be held accountable for their results.

Responsibility is a bedrock concept that has been around for a long time. Although almost everyone recognizes its importance, few people actually know how to create it. This book is our best effort to articulate what it takes to sustain responsibility in the corporate environment. It provides the tools to make responsibility happen.

Responsible managers are not relics from the past; rather, they are the wave of the future. As the pendulum of change in our society moves away from the entitlement mentality and back toward responsibility, they are the leaders who will shape our future. Since responsible managers will be the ones to produce consistent, high-quality results, they will emerge as the indispensable commodity in the corporate world. This book is written to help those who choose to become members of this elite group.

Note

1. Howard Gardner, *Multiple Intelligences: The Theory in Practice* (New York: Basic Books, 1993); Daniel Goleman, *Emotional Intelligence* (New York: Bantam, 1995).

Responsible Managers Get Results

1
Responsibility: Revisited and Redefined

We have asked hundreds of business owners and managers, "Are some people more responsible than others?" The answer is a resounding yes. Interestingly, when people are asked to identify their most responsible colleagues or employees, they are generally able to agree on who the most responsible people are. When we have gone further and asked, "What tells you they are responsible?" we get a variety of answers. But as we look at the answers, some interesting patterns emerge. It becomes obvious that:

- Responsibility is a choice. People either choose to be responsible, or they don't.
- Responsibility means making no excuses.
- Responsibility is not a one-dimensional concept. You can define it only by using two critical dimensions.
- Responsibility is relative. People are judged responsible according to the perspective of those who are doing the judging.

We believe that you can hire for responsibility. You can nurture and coach responsibility. You can develop skills, understanding, and attitudes that make it more likely that responsible people will act responsibly. But as much as managers want responsible workers, they can't make workers responsible. Similarly, workers want responsible leaders, but they can't make their leaders be responsible.

Responsibility Is a Choice

Responsibility starts with the basic understanding that you do in fact have a choice. No matter what the circumstances, you still have the power to choose what you think and what you do. This basic truth is one of the most empowering discoveries a person can make. The power of this understanding is brilliantly revealed in the writings of Victor Frankl,[1] a psychiatrist who was trained in the deterministic tradition of Freudian psychology, which postulates that the events of childhood determine much of our character, personality, and behavior as an adult. But while imprisoned at the Nazi death camp Auschwitz, Frankl had a tremendous insight. At Auschwitz, he and thousands of others underwent horrifying experiences. They were surrounded by death, suffering, and degradation, and had little hope of surviving.

Yet it was there that Frankl began a search for meaning in his life. He looked within himself and found the strength he needed to survive. He writes, "Life ultimately means taking the responsibility to find the right answer to its problems and to fulfill the tasks it constantly sets for each individual."

Frankl watched many in the camp retreat into the past and into despair. But in doing so, they brought no meaning to their current lives. Frankl found his strength in his hopes and dreams for the future. He took the camp's difficulties as a test of his inner strength[2] and found within himself what he would later call "the last of the human freedoms"—the basic freedom that even his Nazi tormentors could not take from him. He had the freedom to choose how to react to all they did to him. No matter what they did, he was still an aware human being with goals, dreams, imagination, conscience, and an independent will. And he realized it was his responsibility to make the most of his life.

From these basic insights he built a personal power. He began to dream, he set goals, he decided what he would do when he was finally free. And he committed himself to not giving in to his captors, to win in the end, and to survive.

Frankl's insights have inspired people for decades. Unlike animals that function on built-in instincts or computers that follow specific programming, human beings have the freedom to choose how they will respond to everything that affects them. We have the freedom to choose what we will think, say, and do. We can decide.

In fact, this insight—if it becomes a driving force in our life, a habit—may be one of the strongest predictors of our success.

Responsibility: The Core of "Emotional Intelligence"

The more we learn about what makes people successful, the more we come to understand the critical role responsibility plays. Responsible people are more successful than their less responsible colleagues at almost everything they do.

For years psychologists and educators have looked to intelligence quotient (IQ) as the great determiner of success. And in fact, study after study has demonstrated that intelligence is a fair predictor of success in most endeavors. But the exceptions to this rule have always puzzled us. Why didn't the class valedictorian end up being one of the most successful? Why do some very mediocre performers on the Scholastic Aptitude Test do so well in college or become such great successes later in their careers?

Partly the answers lie in the statistics used to validate the power of intelligence and our inability to measure other things. Researchers now generally agree that IQ counts for only about 20 percent of the variability in success, so there are bound to be a lot of poor predictions if we use IQ as a predictor.

The recent work on emotional intelligence (EQ) is believed by some to hold promise of producing better predictions. John Mower, the Yale psychologist who coined the term *emotional intelligence*, and Daniel Goleman, who popularized it, describe a variety of qualities that they believe have more power in predicting success in life than does IQ. Goleman states, "When it comes to predicting people's success, braininess as measured by IQ and standardized achievement tests may actually matter less than the qualities of the mind, once thought of as 'character' before the word began to sound quaint."[3] This "character" could also be called "a sense of responsibility." In fact, responsibility may well be at the core of emotional intelligence.

Emotional intelligence includes self-awareness, emotional control, persistence, and the ability to motivate oneself. It also includes an awareness of one's surroundings, empathy, and social deftness.[4] Much of the power of EQ comes from self-awareness and the ability to control emotions (or at least the behavioral outcome of emotions). People who are self-aware have a greater probability of dealing with their emotions. If we know we are angry, at least we can decide whether to deal with it or whether to let it show to others. If we aren't aware of the emotion, it is more likely to go unchecked.

Awareness is a key ingredient in responsibility. To act responsibly, a person must first be aware of her situation and feelings and then exercise her power to control the response.

Self-control is a critical leadership skill. Leaders are generally able to plan and work at a task over a longer time span than those they lead. They have the ability to envision a distant end result or goal, and their commitment to that goal enables them to do what it takes to reach it.

The ability to envision a goal and to control your behavior enough to stay focused on achieving it develops early and is a key ingredient in success. In a study conducted at Stanford University in the 1960s, children were given the following proposal: "If you wait until I run an errand, you can have two marshmallows. If you can't wait, you can have one right now." The children were then left in a room seated at a table. In the middle of the table was that tempting single marshmallow. Some grabbed it. But about two-thirds focused on the goal of two marshmallows. They fought the temptation, covering their eyes or mouths with their hands, biting their lips, or putting their hands behind their back. Some were able to wait fifteen to twenty minutes for the researchers to return. They got their two marshmallows. But even more important, they demonstrated an ability that is a strong predictor of success.

When evaluated twelve to fourteen years later, those who had held out for the two marshmallows proved to be more successful, personally effective, self-assertive, and better able to cope with the challenges of life than those who had given in to temptation. They performed better under stress and were more responsible, self-reliant, and dependable. Their less patient friends, those who had taken the one marshmallow, tended to have more problems and fewer of these desirable qualities. They were more easily frustrated and often more stubborn and indecisive.[5]

The Critical Role of Optimism

Another strong predictor of success that is strongly associated with responsibility is optimism. Martin Seligman, a University of Pennsylvania psychologist, has found that optimism, as measured through an instrument he devised, is a fairly accurate predictor of how well a person will succeed in school, sports, and certain kinds of work. He has had particular success in predicting the success of salespeople with his tests of optimism. Seligman found that when they fail, optimists most often attribute the failure to something they can control, not to some innate weakness that they are helpless to overcome. The optimism to a great extent comes from the person's sense of power over her environment, her confidence in her ability to effect change, even in her own life.[6]

When optimists succeed, they explain it in terms of permanent causes: traits, abilities, personality. Pessimists explain success as based on chance or temporary conditions, feelings, moods, or efforts. Optimists therefore believe good things are likely to happen again. The optimists' confidence is self-reinforcing since it keeps them trying and thinking and problem solving longer than others. A lack of confidence is also self-reinforcing. The salesman who is pessimistic about his sales call and therefore doesn't make the call has no chance to succeed.

At Metropolitan Life, Seligman tracked sales candidates who had taken two tests. One was the company's standard screening instrument, the other Seligman's optimism test. Seligman focused on two groups. One group flunked the standard exam but scored as superoptimists on Seligman's test. The other group were pessimists who passed the standard exam. When it came to sales, the superoptimists outsold the pessimists by 21 percent in the first year and by 57 percent in the second. Met Life has hired optimists for their sales positions ever since.[7]

Both the work on EQ and the work on optimism reinforces our strong belief in the key role of responsibility and provides some insights into its basic underpinnings.

People are more likely to act responsibly when they are self-aware, understand that they do have the power to control their emotional and behavioral responses to the world around them, and believe that they can change the factors that are limiting their success. It may be that both EQ and optimism are driven by responsibility or that people with high EQ and optimism are more likely to be responsible.

Responsibility Means No Excuses

Excuses are the opiate of the unsuccessful. Just as realizing that they have the freedom to choose empowers people, the willingness to make excuses makes them victims. There appears to be a worldwide search for excuses today. People blame the way they are on childhood experiences, a bad teacher, the system, genetics, or a lack of information. The problem with making excuses is that it can become a habit, and once you have the habit it becomes easier to find an excuse than to try hard to change your condition. You become more of a victim than a center of power and influence. You become disempowered.

How many of us have seen great successes come from conditions that others would blame their failure on? In fact, our greatest stories are often about people in the most unlikely situation who overcame all odds and triumphed. From Robert Bruce and White Fang to Rocky our history and literature are filled with inspirational stories of the power of the human will.

A significant part of the modern manager's day is spent attempting to differentiate between excuses and reasons.

"I couldn't get the report done on time because I couldn't get all the members of the team together soon enough."

How would you call it? Did the manager who heard this get an excuse or a reason? The fact is, it really doesn't matter! Either way, the report was late. What we really need in organizations is less effort being expended on justifying failures and more pro-active, responsible thinking about ways of preventing or solving problems and producing results. Falling into the habit of looking for excuses for failure is the real problem. If you heard the preceding comment from someone who generally produces results and is generally a proactive problem solver, you'd probably say it was a reason. From someone else, you might consider it an excuse. But the simple fact is you probably wouldn't hear it from any truly responsible colleague. Responsible people don't waste time on excuses.

One frustrated manager had a number of signs printed that said, "This is an excuse-free work area." He declared September a no-excuses month and told everyone that this month we solve problems, we don't make excuses. When a customer called about a late delivery, the shipping manager said, "You're right, that shipment was late. It won't happen again!" She proceeded to take care of the client by some obvious efforts to make amends. When she hung up, she said she could have come up with several reasons why the shipment was late, but she couldn't use them in no-excuses month. The customer with the late shipment later wrote a letter to the company president commenting on the great service he had received in solving his problem. He said it was refreshing not to get the standard list of excuses and he appreciated the no-nonsense approach that was used.

The habit of making excuses produces people who believe in their helplessness and victimization. If they take responsibility, it is limited to factors they can easily control, things like following orders, completing forms, or managing by the book.

Excuses, pessimism, and helplessness go hand in hand. The excuses are probably the symptom and the pessimism and helplessness the underlying habit and feeling. Whatever the relationship, these elements are generally found together and are the enemies of personal responsibility and, we believe, the enemies of success.

Choosing to blame someone or something for your problems brings some relief—relief from accountability, and relief from facing the challenge of the problem yourself, and relief from acknowledging your contribution to the problem. In other words, by not taking responsibility you disconnect yourself from the world you live in. This act dehumanizes and disempowers you. It represents an act that produces short-term relief and long-term problems. It also helps explain why responsibility is less prevalent than most of us would like. There is difficulty in taking responsibility. When you connect and commit to the world by taking responsibility, you are faced with tough choices and the discomfort that goes with them. The rewards, however, come over the long run in terms of confidence, respect, and a general feeling of empowerment.

Responsibility as Defined on Two Dimensions

From a practical point of view, responsibility can be defined on two dimensions represented by two small words: *to* and *for* (see Figure 1-1). As we mature, we learn that we have responsibility *to* ourselves, our family, our friends, our community, and our

Figure 1-1. Responsibility defined on two dimensions.

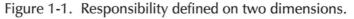

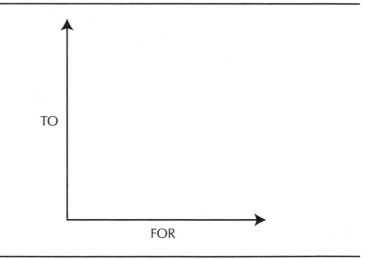

society. We also learn that we are responsible *for* our actions, our words, the use of our talents, those who need our help, and each of the things we own.

When we choose to be responsible to something we commit ourselves to it. This responsibility and commitment are a source of energy that we can apply in the exercise of that responsibility. On this dimension we can choose to take on more or fewer responsibilities. That is, we can choose to take on more or fewer constituencies for our responsibility (see Figure 1-2).

But there are also differing levels of responsibility with respect to each of these constituencies. People may be more or less responsible to themselves, their family, their company, and/or their community. But what makes one person appear to be more responsible on the job than another, or more responsible to his family than another?

Most people think they are responsible. For instance, less responsible people may take responsibility for activities such as showing up, doing their best, or completing the task. People who are pointed out as being more responsible, however, take responsibility for results. They take responsibility for the outcomes of their actions ("Yes, I chopped down the cherry tree")

Figure 1-2. The number of constituencies as a measure of greater or lesser responsibility.

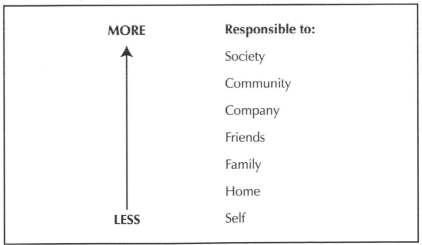

even when the results are less than desirable. And when they know what the goal is, they work hard to achieve it even in the face of great difficulties. Figure 1-3 illustrates the difference between lesser and greater levels of responsibility.

Gerry Faust tells a simple story that helps to bring home this powerful distinction. As a public speaker he has found that an important factor in his success is getting himself and his handout materials to the client on time. In fact, this is so important that Faust Management Corporation has a person in the company whose primary responsibility is getting Gerry and the materials to every event on time and in good condition.

> Recently, I was on my way to a speaking engagement in Toronto. My plane stopped in Chicago and I called the office to check on a few things. As I walked to the phone, I had a horrible déjà vu experience. Eight years before I had been going to this same conference to be the keynote speaker. I had stopped in Chicago then too. I had called the office to talk to Linda, the woman in charge of the handout materials. I asked if my materials had arrived in Toronto. "Don't worry," was the response, "I sent them out six days ago." "Have they gotten there yet?" I asked. "I sent them Federal Express. They are guaranteed to be there in two days" was the not so reassuring reply.

Figure 1-3. The greater sense of responsibility shown by people who hold themselves accountable for results.

Responsible

Less   More

Activities   Results

Responsible for

Let's analyze this conversation. Or rather, let's analyze these two conversations since there are really two different conversations here. One is a conversation about activities, the other is about results.

Surely Linda felt responsible. She felt responsible for getting the right information (address, date, contact person, number and type of materials). She probably felt responsible for choosing the right shipping container, packing the box to protect the materials, and getting it to Federal Express early enough to allow some cushion for a timely delivery. But, as the conversation shows, she had not followed through to ensure results. Gerry continues his story.

> That was eight years ago. And with the memory of that former phone call running through my mind, I approached the new phone call with some trepidation. When I reached my assistant, Amy, I asked, "Are my materials there yet?" "Yes, Alicia got them three days ago," she said, "but when I called she told me there would be 400 extra people at the speech. Don't worry, though, she's gotten the extras too. In fact, she seemed a bit unsure about the number so I asked her if the number was fixed. She said not exactly because people can register at the door. Given this, I was afraid that 400 wouldn't be enough, so I sent 600 just to be safe. By the way, she asked me if you wanted the materials handed out ahead of time. I told her usually you do. But since this is a new speech, I wasn't sure. So we agreed that she will hand them out ahead of time, unless you tell her not to. I have her phone number where she can be reached tonight, if you want her to do something different."

Here's a simple question: Which of these two women, Amy or Linda, would you like to have working for you? The answer is obvious: You would like Amy, and so would Gerry. Gerry can rest easy when Amy's on the job because she takes responsibility for results. She knows that results are critical and she won't rest until she delivers them.

Results vs. Activities

Leaders generally agree that they want people to take responsibility for results. And they generally agree that their greatest frustrations come from people who focus their responsibility on activities. The problem is that too many managers manage as though they want people to be responsible for activities rather than results. If we really wanted to focus on results, our job descriptions would focus on the results we want from a position and not on the activities involved in it. The comments we make to subordinates would focus on helping them to produce results more than on the activities they are engaged in. And the training we do would focus on the results we want, how to evaluate whether we've achieved them, and then and only then on activities that "usually" lead to those results. Even more important, we would focus our hiring activities on finding out about the character of the people we're considering. We would try to assess their understanding of the importance of results, maybe their EQ or level of optimism or ability to handle discomfort in the pursuit of goals. We would determine who are the results producers. We certainly would not focus primarily on the activities they have been involved with in the past. Unfortunately, all too few of these statements are descriptive of common management practice.

If we want to have a responsible organization, we have to change the way we hire and focus management on developing the skills, attitudes, and abilities that form the foundation of responsibility. We have to hire and develop people who are prepared to change their activities when they realize that the desired results aren't happening.

More responsible people take on responsibility to many constituencies other than themselves. They are not satisfied with taking responsibility only for activities; they want to take responsibility for results. In fact, truly responsible people aren't very happy if they are only given responsibility for activities. It takes them out of the game and does not allow them to be creative, exercise judgment, make decisions, or feel that they've really made a contribution.

Responsible people need to know what results you're after. Then all you have to do is get out of their way. At the start of the Spanish-American War, the president of the United States wanted to secure the cooperation of the Cuban insurgents. The problem was how to get a message to their leader, Garcia, who was somewhere in the Cuban mountains. The president was told, "If anyone can get a message to Garcia, Lieutenant Andrew Rowan can." Rowan took the letter, sealed it in an oilskin pouch, and four days later landed in an open boat on the Cuban coast. He then plunged into the jungle disguised as an English sportsman. Three weeks later, he came out on the other side of the island, mission accomplished.[8]

When given his task, Rowan didn't ask questions. He saluted and got on with it. How he was able to succeed given the odds is one of the great wonders of that war.

Throughout the world there are leaders who would like to have a Rowan working for them—someone who does not complain, who does not even wait for full instructions. But someone they can count on to carry their "message to Garcia."

Levels of Responsibility

Responsible people take responsibility for results for all of those they choose to be responsible to, including themselves. Figure 1-4 represents our findings and beliefs about the importance of the words "to" and "for" and their relation to differing levels of responsibilities.

What Figure 1-4 summarizes is that most people are somewhat responsible. Most are responsible to themselves in the sense that they don't do things that are dangerous, they eat regularly and get enough sleep. But some are more responsible. They realize that their life is what they make of it. No matter what the obstacles, they are responsible for their own happiness and their own success. They do not make excuses.

We have all seen siblings who have been raised in the same home with the same parents, have the same general opportunities, and maybe even similar levels of innate intelligence or talent

Figure 1-4. The greater responsibility for results in many areas of their lives taken by more responsible people.

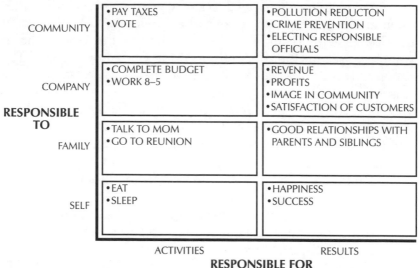

	ACTIVITIES	RESULTS
	RESPONSIBLE FOR	

who nevertheless grow up to be very different people. One may be dependent and depressed, the other independent and excited about all the opportunity in the world. One blames the past for his difficulties, the other makes opportunities out of adversity, lemonade out of lemons. Both people are exercising some degree of responsibility to themselves, but one is obviously very much more responsible.

For each person or group we choose to be responsible to we can be more or less responsible depending on whether we are prepared to take responsibility for the results that are important to them. In a family, one child may call Mom regularly, go to family reunions, and do a variety of things to demonstrate responsibility to the family. Meanwhile, another exercises even more responsibility by doing whatever it takes to make sure there is a good relationship between himself and his brothers and sisters, works hard to help the others get opportunities or to succeed, and in general does what it takes to create the results that define the success of a family.

In organizations some people work 9 to 5, participate in the budgeting process, conduct training programs, and answer customers' questions. Someone else, who is more responsible, arrives on time ready to work, works to ensure that the budget is realistic and will result in the goals being met, works with a training course participant until she truly understands, and conducts a program so well that enrollment doubles and participants rave about it. This kind of person not only answers the customer's questions but also takes time to make sure that the customer understands and is satisfied with the answer, and does it all in a way that brings a level of magic to the encounter.

The community example is similar. We have all known people who go through the motions of citizenship, and we have all known some who go the extra mile. They work to learn about and to inform others about issues and candidates. They help establish the recycling program and are active in a neighborhood watch program. They campaign for officials and policies they believe in. They work for and act and feel responsible for the "success" of their community.

Responsible leaders focus their colleagues' attention on results. They get them to understand that the results, not the activities, are the defining characteristics of great performance. Responsible managers and workers focus on the desired results and will not rest until they have achieved them.

The casual judgments within organizations seem to focus heavily on evaluating people in terms of whether they take responsibility for results. This happens because within these contexts the responsibility "to" dimension is relatively fixed. That is, there is some agreement on whom people should be responsible to. However, to truly evaluate and develop responsibility requires a much deeper understanding of both dimensions of this powerful concept.

Responsibility and Maturity

Many believe that responsibility is the result of maturity. It is probably more true that it is the cause of maturity. Those who are responsible are mature regardless of their age.

On the "to" dimension, maturity is very much associated with accepting responsibility to others. We all start out as newborns responsible only to ourselves and maintain a "me-centered" view of the universe until about age 2. Then just when we are really getting to enjoy the idea that the world is set up for us, we begin to hear those frightful words "No, that belongs to your sister!" By age 2, people around us get serious about reinforcing the idea of responsibility to others. The responsibilities build up slowly at first. There's the responsibility to siblings, parents, friends, and to the family and its possessions. As we grow older the list lengthens. There are more friends, the football or soccer team, the school or religious institution, and later the job, the spouse, the children, the in-laws, the volunteer organizations, and the community.

Unfortunately, few responsibilities drop off as new ones are added. Even that early responsibility to self must be maintained. Mature people are and should be responsible to themselves. We should concern ourselves with how well we're being taken care of in our jobs and relationships.

Over time the challenge becomes balancing all the constituencies of our responsibility. Often our responsibilities to others compete with one another and with our responsibility to ourselves. We stay late at work to complete an important project even though we'd like to be working out or at home with the family.

Have you ever thought that your responsibilities have gone too far? That just maybe you are now responsible to too many others? Don't feel alone!! This is a common feeling of many people who carry a heavy burden of responsibility. Often the load could be made lighter if only these people would nurture responsibility and empower others. The executive who tries to be a superwoman, who manages an executive career, is active in the PTA and other civic projects, and is also a loving wife and mother of four children can try to do it all alone. But unless she is working for a dramatic, awe-inspiring epitaph, we suggest a little delegation, more sharing of her responsibilities. She can accept responsibility in these many areas but will be better off sharing some of the duties.

The same could be said for the supermanager. Remember, as you take on new responsibilities, you should try to shed old ones. This doesn't mean that you should walk away from them.

Rather, you should plan to develop others who will have the capability to and are prepared to take on your old responsibilities as you take on new ones.

The president of an East Coast manufacturing company was describing his hectic life and some challenges in the accounting reports. He was asked, "What does the chief financial officer say about that?" He replied, "I am the CFO." "What about the chief information officer?" was the next question. "I'm also the CIO" was his answer. This very responsible, dedicated, second-generation president of a $30-million company still held every job he had ever had in the company since he joined it. He was given this advice: "You need to learn how to develop others and give away jobs."

How many people do you know who have trouble developing others and nurturing and delegating responsibility? These skills along with setting personal goals and priorities are critical for people with a well-developed sense of responsibility.

People also mature on the "for" dimension of responsibility. As children, we generally do as we are told or copy what others do. As we grow and our ability to assess situations, make decisions, and solve problems increases, we have more potential to take responsibility for results. We have the skills and insights to become more proactive.

This critical relationship between responsibility and our ability to assess (to be self-aware, observe, and interpret what we see, hear, and feel), to make decisions relative to what we are sensing and what actions we should take, and to solve problems is a central theme of this book. At some point, the tasks we are given or are expected to perform involve uncertainty and judgment. They cannot be completed successfully just by following rules, protocols, and procedures.

The challenge of work (and of life in general) is to achieve results whatever the obstacles. It requires persistence, perspective, and judgment. Leaders win when they delegate to people who will take responsibility for the results. The willingness to take on and the ability to complete tasks when the desired results are defined but the way to achieve them is unclear are defining characteristics of the people we regularly call responsible.

Responsibility Is Relative

Most people believe that more responsible people take on more responsibility to others. However, in reality, being responsible to more constituencies does not necessarily mean that we are being more responsible. Sometimes giving up some of our responsibility to one or more of our constituencies is the most responsible thing to do.

The highly successful business executive who spends long hours at work, is forever on the road, and regularly misses family events may be considered less responsible by his or her spouse and children, while the chairman of the board may see the same person as very responsible.

People judge the responsibility of others by whom (or what) they are responsible *to* and what they take responsibility *for*. The judgment is relative to what the person doing the judging believes others should be responsible to and for. If you appear to be responsible to those I believe you should be responsible to, and if you take responsibility for what I believe you should take responsibility for, I will judge you as being responsible.

Notice that my judgment regarding your responsibility can be affected by a number of things. These include:

- The congruence between my beliefs regarding responsibility (to and for) and my interpretation of your behavior
- The congruence between your feelings of responsibility (to and for), the decisions you make, and your behavior
- The congruence of my beliefs regarding responsibility (to and for) and yours

In an organization a good place to start developing responsibility is to get people on the same wavelength regarding whom or what to be responsible to and what to be responsible for.

Responsibility in Organizations

Organizations should never expect to be the focus of all of a person's responsibility. The best employees maintain a sense of balance. They are responsible to their family, their friends, their religious group, the PTA, and so on. The best a company can hope for is its fair share of the responsibility of their people. But to get the value from that responsibility, it must be focused. And the focus should be on two primary constituencies: the customer and the organization.

Responsibility to the customer is important because it is the customers and their needs that define the purpose of the organization. Organizations that don't continue to develop their understanding of their customers and markets, and don't act responsibly to those customers and markets, lose their relevance and often lose their shirts.

Responsibility to the organization provides a balance to the responsibility to the customer. In fact, the responsible manager or worker strives to create results that the customer wants and that the organization wants. The difficult balance comes when the customer wants the product at no charge and the organization wants to make a profit. Satisfying the customers' needs becomes the driving goal. But we must serve their needs as best we can while living within the constraints of the company's goals. Note that we didn't say the company's policies and procedures. This would be okay as long as those policies and procedures were consistent with achieving both customer goals and company goals. Unfortunately, this is not always the case. Certainly if everything is set up right, serving the needs of the customer is also in the best interests of the company. However, the company does have its own needs and therefore must be considered separately.

Responsibility to the Employee

There is a third area of responsibility that is important for those who lead: responsibility to the employees. People are a critical resource to any organization. But because the particular focus of this book is on developing a responsible workforce, we have addressed this area of responsibility only indirectly in terms of its relationship to responsibility to the organization and to the customers. Since responsibility is a choice, leaders must produce the results the employees want (that is, must be responsible to employees) if they want their people to choose to be responsible to the organization and if they want them to choose on a day-to-day basis to be responsible to the customer. There is ample evidence that the best customer service and in fact the best performance in general comes from involved, appreciated, and fulfilled employees. Since we find that responsibility to the employee is part of building responsibility to the customer and the organization, we have chosen to address its key elements under those topics in Chapters 2 and 3.

Results for Customers and Organizations

Throughout the business world, the focus on results is growing. And the reason for this is simple. Results are getting harder to come by. In simpler times, the results just seemed to happen for many people: The post–World War II expanding economy and expanding marketplace covered a multitude of sins and made many fools look like heroes. It takes more difficult times to separate the superior managers from their less capable competitors.

We believe we have seen a watershed shift in the business world. Success is more difficult to achieve and maintain today than ever before, and it's likely to stay that way. The reason is simple. Many things have changed. Customers are becoming more sophisticated and more demanding, competition is increasing, and everyone is becoming more efficient. Business is becoming more global. Product life cycles are much shorter. Time to market is decreasing, and a given advantage cannot be held for very long. Competition puts pressure on margins. Customers' demands put pressures on quality, cost of goods, and cost of sale. Put all this together and it becomes increasingly difficult to achieve the results and the success that shareholders, owners, and businesses demand. Businesses are having to become more efficient, to do more with less. Organizations are being reorganized, reinvented, and reengineered all over the globe in the desperate search for better results.

With all this activity, then, and with all we supposedly know about training and people and organizations, why is it that we are having such difficulty creating the right results? How do you build an organization in which managers and employees choose to be responsible to the organization and to its customers and for the results that both the customer and the organization want and need? *And* in which they have the skills, knowledge, understanding, perspective, and desire needed to deliver those results? This question is the focus of the remaining chapters of this book.

Notes

1. Victor Frankl, *Man's Search for Meaning* (Boston: Beacon Press, 1962).
2. Ibid.
3. Daniel Goleman, *Emotional Intelligence* (New York: Bantam Books, 1995).
4. Ibid.
5. Ibid.
6. Martin Seligman, *Learned Optimism* (New York: Pocket Books, 1990).
7. Ibid.
8. Elbert Hubbard, "A Message to Garcia," *The Philistine* (1899).

2

Building Responsibility
to the Customer

Organizations exist to fill the needs of their customers. Without the customers, we have no purpose. The need for leadership and management is derived from this purpose. Leaders and managers emerge only when there is a goal, and when the job of achieving it is too much for one person to handle alone. Consider the following story, which can teach us a lot about leadership, management, and responsibility.

> Five people set out to go over a mountain. As they walk they move into the foothills, then onto the mountain. As they climb, the path narrows. They find themselves with a 2,000-foot chasm on one side and a 500-foot cliff on the other. Suddenly, they encounter a rock that blocks their path. The rock is a big one, far too big for any one of them alone to move.

Question 1:
If this group of people is truly committed to going over the mountain, what will happen?

You guessed it! Management will happen. Leadership will happen. There may also be some conflict, some teamwork, and some creativity.

Question 2:
What caused these interesting things to happen?

Right again! The rock caused these interesting

things to happen. Why? It focused the energy and effort of the group. Until they encountered the rock, they were just on a hike.

Every organization has a "rock," something that brings people together, that becomes the focus of their collective effort, the focus of their responsibility. The rock of organizations is best defined by a set of needs of a group of people we call customers. Serving the needs of the customer is the raison d'être of any organization. Whether it be a museum or a candy store, a multinational conglomerate or a sidewalk café, all organizations have customers, and how well the organization succeeds depends in large measure on how well those customers' needs are met.

We can learn even more about the challenge of organizational leadership and management if we go back to the mountain to see how our hikers are doing with their rock.

It is now seven hours since the five climbers encountered the rock. Because this is a well-traveled path, there are now over 1,100 people lined up behind the rock. There are eight people feverishly working on moving the rock, one person who can't get to the rock but is offering lots of advice (obviously, this one's a manager), another who is at a bend in the path and can see both the rock and the long line of people. She has decided to direct traffic and has asked one of the workers to rest, while signaling to a large fellow from farther back in the line to come forward. At the end of the line is a fellow who is concerned about the group and has decided to take orders and run to town for sandwiches. Here are some more questions:

Question 3:
If you went to the back of the line and asked, "What are we doing here?" what answer would you get?

Probably a variety of answers. Here are some possibilities:

- *I don't know.* I have never known and don't really expect to know in the future. I just show up every day and the line is here.

- *We're going for lunch.* (This, from the guy who is taking orders, shows a common belief: What I am doing is what we're doing.)
- *We're having a picnic!* (This from a deep thinker who puts together the idea of lunch and the outdoors.)
- *We're starting a catering business.* (This from the entrepreneurial friend of the guy taking the orders.)

Question 4:
How many of the 1,100 people would know anything about the rock?

Probably only a few of the many people on the mountain know about the rock. If you ask about the rock, you are likely to get a blank stare, a shoulder shrug, and an offhand, "What rock?"

Doing the Job but Forgetting the Customer

Many organizations are like the 1,100 people on the mountain. Some people are working on the rock, while others are having a picnic. Only a few truly understand the nature of the problem even though all are busy in the enterprise. You could develop much greater commitment in most organizations if you took more of the people up to the front of the line and let them see and touch the rock. We define the rock of organizations by the results customers want.

But in the scramble of all you do each day, is it easy to forget about the rock? Be careful: We're not talking about theoretical "shoulds" here, we're talking about practical "do's." The practical answer is generally yes. It's very easy to forget about the customers and their needs because there is so much to do. In fact, there are many powerful forces that regularly distract us from the customer. Not the least of these is our jobs.

A business executive suffering the effects of a long overnight plane ride walks slowly into the lobby of a large, classy hotel. It is 6:00 A.M., and the reception staff is busily preparing for the morning's checkouts. They have just received instructions from the night shift and are preparing packets for a large group that will be checking in later that day. That is their job. As the weary customer approaches, he notices the intensity with which they are doing their jobs. No one looks up to greet him. He stands at the counter for what seems like hours before he clears his throat, drops his bag with a crash, and finally says, "Can you help me?"

He later reflects, "I'm sure they have a policy in this hotel that reads 'If you don't have eye contact with a guest you don't have to serve them.'" That is his only explanation for the intensity with which those people avoided looking up until they were done with their appointed tasks.

Many retail stores and the ticketing and gate personnel of many airlines must have the same policy. Every day, people around the world work diligently at their jobs and ignore their customers. The more demanding the job, the easier it is to do so. We must break this habit if we are to build customer-responsible organizations. We must get all of our people to know and understand the rock, and we must build a raging river of customer responsibility throughout the organization.

Building a River of Responsibility

Think of the power of a river. That power comes from the volume of water, the pull of gravity, and the focus provided by the riverbanks. The volume of water comes from many small sources, all running in the same direction. The pull of gravity provides drive and force as the water moves toward its goal, the ocean. The banks provide boundaries that concentrate the flow and give it more force and power.

Unfortunately, many organizations are more like puddles or lakes than powerful rivers. They may be tranquil and peaceful, but they aren't going anywhere. They do not collect and concentrate the efforts of the entire organization, or have the pull of a clear sense of purpose, or the boundaries needed to focus their efforts to allow them to go over and around, under or through, the obstacles they encounter.

To build a powerful river of responsibility to customers in your organization you must follow these steps:

1. Get everyone committed to producing the results customers want.
2. Provide focus by:
   a. Carefully selecting the customers and needs you will serve
   b. Creating strategies that focus on providing value to select customers
   c. Aligning structures, systems, processes, and culture with the strategy
3. Get everyone involved in improving value to the customer and managing each customer interaction.

Commitment to the Customer

More and more companies are realizing that the following are critical differentiators in the ever more competitive marketplace: their focus on the customer, and the resulting focus on their positioning, improvement in customer relations, and quality of product and service.

This focus on the customer is like a growing wave in businesses around the world, taking many forms and found in writings from authors with very different perspectives. Salespeople are focusing on collaborative selling, getting to know customers' needs, and then matching what they have with what the customer wants. Strategists and market researchers are turning from a numbers-focused approach to approaches that are more customer-focused. The focus today is on positioning, differentiation, and one-to-one marketing. And people who have focused on manufacturing efficiencies, product quality, and organizational culture are telling us to get out of the office or off the shop floor to talk to our customers.

Focus on Customers and Service

During the 1980s, the concepts of customer focus and customer service took their place among the hot topics of management. Books like *Moments of Truth*[1] and *Service America*[2] led the charge, which has been followed by a plethora of books that have told us how to create customers for life, customer-intimate relationships, and Total Quality Service.

There has been a subtle shift that has brought businesses closer to their customers over the past twenty-five years. This is reflected in the book titles and methodologies that have been popular during that period. The focus initially appeared to be on how to manipulate customers, with titles like *Sell and Grow Rich*, *The Secrets of Closing the Sale*, *How to Close Every Sale*, and *How to Sell Anything to Anybody*. What to do and what to say to get them to buy were the tricks of the trade. The manipulative aspect of these approaches was so strong that one team of authors, concerned about the trend, entitled their book *Non-Manipulative Selling*. Alessandra, Wexler, and Barrera focused primarily on how to understand a customer and the process of needs-based or collaborative selling.[3] Since the 1980s the shift has been away from manipulating customers and toward giving customers what they want and meeting or, better yet, exceeding their expectations.

The most recent books have focused even more on developing commitment to and relationships with customers. We believe the next step is understanding that successful organizations and successful businesspeople are those who accept responsibility to the customer and who take responsibility for producing the results customers want.

Producing Results Customers Want

The first step in building a customer-responsible organization is for people to understand the purpose of the organization and its intimate relationship to the customers and their needs. The second is to create a constant quest for understanding who the customers are, how they think, and what makes a difference to them, leading to an intimate knowledge of the customers whom the business must serve day to day.

First let's take a look at some basic tenets of customer service.

Customers' Evaluation of the Total Experience

If there is one tenet that underlies enlightened management philosophies regarding customers, it is that it is the customers' definition of quality that matters. And if we are learning anything, it is that there is a lot that matters to most customers.

Customers evaluate the quality of those who supply their product or service on the basis of the total experience they have with them. That experience includes the advertising; the phone calls; how they are treated before, during, and after the sale; the product (through its life span); and all follow-through and maintenance activities.

Once we hired a company to trim the trees at our office. They were supposed to remove a tree that grew out of the center of a turnaround driveway and fill in the hole with asphalt. In addition, they agreed to remove the stump of another tree that had fallen over in a recent storm. They offered to do the job at a good price, had a crew on the job the next day, and worked quickly. The trees they trimmed looked good. But they left without taking care of the asphalt and the stump. It took twenty-seven days of phone calls before they filled the hole and removed the stump, and we became less and less satisfied with their tree trimming work each day. Needless to say, we never recommend that company.

Since the product/service package varies so from business to business, it is hard to talk in generalities. However, there are some basic principles:

1. *To assess the value of what you offer you must consider all aspects of the product/service package.* The product/service package includes all the things and experiences that customers use to form an impression of the value they have received.

2. *Value is determined in the mind of the customer.* Customers regularly make decisions about the value they receive. These de-

cisions determine their impression of the organizations they deal with. They determine how they rate your company relative to your competition and whether they will remain your customer.

3. *Value is relative.* The value determination of customers is based on their expectations. High expectations make average performance look bad; low expectations make average performance look good.

What Customers Value

Some of what customers want can be identified in societal and business trends. There is a time in the development of most economies when anyone who has a product can be successful. In such times, demand exceeds supply and competition is limited. Today's Western markets, by contrast, are characterized by heavy competition and a frenetic drive to find a competitive edge. Most businesses realize that it takes their customers only a few minutes to find another supplier. They let their fingers do the walking and then the dialing, and you can be replaced before the next delivery is due.

Our current competitive marketplace is one in which the customer has tremendous power. More and more, they are prepared to exercise that power. Customers have learned that they don't have to settle for much, if anything, of what they are offered. They can demand more. To help us understand what customers are looking for, let's explore a couple of growing trends that are likely to have a large impact on most markets over the next decade.

The Value Placed on Customization

Customers want something special, something just for them. You need only look at the success of Starbucks and microbreweries to see the trend.

The coffee industry of the 1970s and 1980s was dominated by a few big players, and although coffee consumption was growing, the focus of the industry was on low-cost production and providing greater flavor faster (for instance, instant coffee) in a fast-food world. Coffee was definitely a commodity product. Then came the gourmet coffee explosion. Who would have believed that so many people would be willing to pay up to $4.00 for a cup of coffee? But the fact is that people really will pay a premium to get exactly what they want and to be made to feel special.

Starbucks changed the industry trend from trying to figure out how to lower the price of a cup of coffee to figuring out how to create so much value that people would gladly pay more. They obviously succeeded.

The beer industry has followed a similar pattern. The 1960s and 1970s can be characterized as a time of consolidation. The number of brewing companies was cut by more than 60 percent as the big got bigger and the small, local, and regional operations were swallowed up. But the pendulum swung back in the 1990s. Microbreweries and microbeers proliferated. There are now beer-of-the-month clubs and specialty stores with row after row of exotic beers.

Even the biggest players are now coming out with their microbeer look-alike brands so that they can compete in the specialty market. The point is, there are no more mass markets. To be sure, there are no more customers who want to be treated like mass market customers. To compete in today's marketplace and to be able to deliver the results customers want, you have to know your customers and know them very well. You have to understand the microsegments in your markets and better yet know your customers as individuals. And you have to be prepared to customize your product so that the customer knows you made it just for him.

The Value Placed on Time

Closely related to the growing demand for a customized product/service package is the growing demand for product at my place, product at my time, and product with no hassles. Of course we really mean the right product/service package where the customer wants it, when she wants it, and without any hassle. These forms of customization are derived from an underlying search for convenience driven by an increasing understanding of the value of time. People's lives are getting more complex and congested and their workdays are longer and longer.

Flexible or discretionary time for most people is a disappearing commodity. No wonder, then, that they put such a high value on their time. No wonder that they don't want to waste those precious hours driving to the restaurant or the store, standing in line, filling out forms, or waiting for service. And no wonder that they don't want to have their schedules dictated by the working hours of their suppliers.

It is interesting that the home delivery market is growing again. The catalogue business, once in decline, has had a great resurgence. The great catalogue companies like L.L. Bean, Lands' End, and Cabella's have looked carefully at what and when people buy. They have studied what their customers want and how they define quality and service. You can now order guaranteed quality merchandise twenty-four hours a day with a toll-free phone call or a fax, and it can be delivered the next day.

The Home Shopping Network and the Internet have allowed people to order from the couch or to "surf the store." The cable shopping shows and infomercials sell millions of dollars worth of products every day.

The focus on convenience and the value of time has not only found its legs in home-delivered products and services; it has also resulted in changes in ticketing for airlines. Business travelers hardly see the ticket counter these days, and if it weren't for security checks, they would probably be walking directly onto planes with their electronic tickets.

Managing the Moments of Truth

Probably few concepts have had a greater impact on our understanding of customer service than "moments of truth." In his book of that title, Jan Carlzon described his experience as he tried to revitalize Scandinavian Airlines (SAS) and his insights into this concept. The book's key premises include:

- The overall reputation of a business is determined by the outcome of hundreds or thousands of moments of truth.
- These moments of truth involve a customer interacting with that business.
- The outcome is related to whether the person's expectations are met or not.

Each moment of truth can have one of three potential outcomes depending on how well or poorly the customer's expectations have been met.

1. *A neutral moment.* A situation in which the customer's expectations are met—no more, no less. The customer is satisfied. He got what he wanted. His impression of the organization may be reinforced, but it is not changed.

2. *A moment of magic.* A situation in which the customer's expectations are noticeably exceeded. He is surprised (or delighted) with what he received. His impression of the organization improves, and he is likely to tell a couple of friends about it. He becomes what some have called a raving fan.[4]

3. *A moment of misery.* A situation in which the customer's expectations are noticeably not met. He is disappointed and, if severely so, likely to tell several friends and even a couple of mere acquaintances about his dissatisfaction.[5]

The name of the game in business is to reduce the misery and increase the magic. The reason why this concept of moments of truth is so powerful is that it creates a focus for the frontline person on the critical situations—those times when she is face to face with the customer or communicating with or serving him in some way. Recognizing the time when opportunity is present, when good judgment, creativity, and the proper decision can really pay off, is important for all of us. All too often we let these critical moments pass by unnoticed in the hours of trying to get everything done. But this is a concept that can have an impact at all levels of an organization.

For frontline sales and servicepeople who deal with customers every day, it's critical. But it's just as important to the receptionist, the bookkeeping staff, and the cleanup crew. All have their moments of truth, their moments of opportunity.

Creating Magic

Having people view a video or a role play or read a story and count the moments of truth they can spot in them is the start of an interesting exercise. But recognizing the moments of truth is not enough. The real challenge is in how you actually create magic and avoid misery. Training in magic making can be elaborate, but it can also be short and fun. Having people view a video or a role play and discuss what they could do to create magic will work. So will having a "moment of magic" contest to give people a chance to report on their efforts to create magic. Or if you want a good start to a meeting, simply begin to tell moments of magic stories. The more of these story-telling sessions there are and the farther down the organization they go, the better. The important thing is that people need to be able to:

- Recognize moments of truth for what they are.
- Be creative in finding new ways to give more service or to increase the value of the product/service package.
- Judge an event. Is it likely to create magic or isn't it?

It does not generally cost money to create magic, and it generally pays very big dividends in free publicity and customer retention. O'Brien Glass, one of the dominant players in the automobile and flat glass industry in Australia, launched a "moments of magic" campaign in the late 1980s. It started with a cross-Australia seminar tour in which the basics were introduced, followed by video training sessions conducted by branch managers. There were contests and special incentives. One unique element was that servicepeople could create magic by identifying customers' needs and actually selling a product. The servicepeople carried colorful stickers to put on glass doors where children were in the house, provided free inspections of windows, and tightened screens. When they found a sliding glass door that wasn't made of safety glass, they pointed out the danger and offered a reduced price for installing the safety glass there and then. The lower price reflected the savings of another "house call."

The program was so successful that it resulted in record sales growth and was repeated in modified form for three years. The moments of magic theme is now an integrated part of the O'Brien Glass culture, and it has helped keep the company a profitable, growing service leader in its industry for years.

O'Brien Glass and many others have had great success because they drew some important logical inferences from the moments of truth concept.

- The greatest opportunity for magic comes when expectations are low. Therefore, being able to manage the customer interaction when there is a problem is a critical skill for those who manage the moments of truth.
- Most of the moments of truth are not under the control of senior managers. They involve the frontline workers, the receptionists, the accountants, the service providers.
- If the workers are handling the moments of truth, they need the skills, attitudes, understanding, and authority to create magic and avoid misery.

These last two points are among the strongest arguments for frontline empowerment.

The first point drove the SAS "moments of truth" program. When doing the research to determine what they had to do to create magic for their customers, Carlson's SAS did a unique thing. SAS asked its customers what mattered to them! SAS discovered many things with this approach. One of the most interesting was that customers regularly pointed to one factor as being very important. This factor had not occurred to the researchers before the study and certainly not to the hundreds of people making up customer satisfaction surveys before them. What customers really wanted was help when things went wrong. Even more, when they had problems, they wanted to be able to talk to people who acted as if they cared.

The message is simple: When an angry, frustrated customer is in front of you, act as if you care! Even if it's two minutes before closing time, even if you really can't help, even if you're embarrassed about what happened or don't like the way the customer is yelling, ACT AS IF YOU CARE!!

The caring starts with listening and showing that you understand. Remain calm, tell the customer she has come to the right place and you are the right person, and you will take action to correct the situation. Then ask the person to help you understand the facts and what she would like you to do to correct the situation. But in the end, you show the customer you care by doing something, preferably something special that shows you'll go out of your way. You'll stop doing your "job" and you will take care of her. The more you go out of your way, the more effort you expend, the more magic you'll create.[6]

Responsibility to the customer starts with caring—caring enough to ensure that the customer understands you care and that the customer gets the results she wants and needs.

Cycles of Service

Moments of truth often come in bunches. In fact, a series of moments of truth is generally strung together whenever a customer deals with you. This string of moments of truth has been defined as a cycle of service, which has a defined beginning and end.[7] It starts when a customer presents herself to your organization to do business, and it ends when the customer considers the service complete. For example, a business executive checks into a luxury hotel. A smiling doorman says, after looking at the name tags on her bags, "Good morning, Ms. Walters. Good to have you with us." He then takes her inside and introduces her to the person at the reception counter. The executive checks in, and a bellman accompanies her to her room, where she opens the curtains, takes a deep breath, and admires the cityscape before her.

All of these individual moments constitute a cycle of service. But they are part of a broader cycle of service that ends only when she checks out. And the customer's impression of that entire cycle of service could be colored by the outcome of any of the component moments of truth.

A bad encounter with the person at the reception desk or with a room service waiter, or a TV set that won't work and doesn't get fixed, and the entire experience can get painted with the misery brush. On the other hand, if the whole experience is satisfactory and any (or all) of the hotel staff creates a moment of real magic, the whole cycle of service might just make it into the magic category.

Analyzing a business to identify its critical cycles of service and working to ensure that there is lots of magic and very little misery in each is a sound activity for companies trying to develop responsibility to the customer.

Market Research

To give you the real in-depth answers you need if you are going to create a customer-responsible organization, look to your customers, potential customers, and former customers. There are many important questions they can answer, but all too few businesses take the time to ask. There are different reasons to go to the customer and at least as many methods for doing it. Let's consider a few.

Market research can take a number of forms. It can include the gathering of data to:

- Size markets (to discover how many potential skiers there are between ages 16 and 23 in Nebraska, for instance)
- Identify market or demographic trends (youth soccer is growing faster than football)
- Identify market segments (the out-of-condition market has needs that differ from those of the health club hard bodies)
- Analyze competitors (Absolutely American has been positioned to attack the Clearly Canadian brand)
- Identify key targets (Pacificare has more Medicare patients than any other group in southern California so it should be the first target for our new knee replacement alternative)

Market research helps you to think and build strategy and to manage many of your efforts. It is critical, but it is not the whole answer. Customer research (or customer perception or customer-defined quality research) goes even further. It helps you to understand what the customer feels, wants, expects, hates, and values the most. It helps you to understand the reasons customers buy, the reasons they come back, and the reasons they leave you or prefer someone else.

Unfortunately, as commonly done, market and customer research is usually too structured. It is too narrowly focused on products that we already have or can think of or asks only for an evaluation of how we are doing.

The more structured a data-gathering process is, the more it depends on your knowing everything before you start. Generally, open-ended questions, focus groups, and interviews are better than multiple choice or rating scale questionnaires because they can help you learn what you don't know.

Product-related research might ask if you like product or package A better than product or package B. Although this may help you to refine your product or packaging, it doesn't necessarily tell you what would really turn the customer on.

The customer satisfaction questionnaire is one of the least useful and most overused research tools. It may be good to set a baseline or to measure the effectiveness of a new program or service and can give you some assistance in deciding that check-in procedures and baggage handling are your weakest areas. But it doesn't often help you to decide what to do differently. It is good for measuring your organization but not much good for developing an in-depth understanding of the customers.

To build customer-responsible organizations, we need to get more people to understand more intimately what our customers want and what makes them happy, sad, buy, leave, or tick. Here are three suggestions:

1. Get your people face to face with real customers, ex-customers, noncustomers, and potential customers.
2. Design research that involves some structure and much dialogue.
3. Ask questions that probe feelings and customers' sense of relative value.
   • If we could do one thing better, what would you like it to be?

- What does Harry's Laundry do better than we do?
- When you are choosing a hotel, what three things would you like to know about it before you decide to stay there?
- If you could have the pizza faster or bigger, which would you prefer?
- What do you like most about doing business with us?

In his book *The Only Thing That Matters*, Karl Albrecht identifies four basic types of questions you can ask to find out what customers value:

1. What attributes of the customer experience are of particular value?
2. How desirable is each attribute relative to the others?
3. How well do we score, compared with relevant competition, on each of these factors that are most valued?
4. What can we do to add value to the customer experience and therefore provide a differentiated or breakaway service?[8]

We have found that you get a triple advantage when these questions are asked by the people providing the service, manufacturing the product, or doing the accounting. First, your people meet the customer and can feel the warmth or the heat. They can touch the rock. Second, they can ask the other questions that make the information more meaningful or that help them decide what "we" can do to increase "our" value. Third, you get the customer-oriented data you need. The face-to-face experience can be in focus groups or one-on-one interviews. When you are trying to build responsibility, there is nothing better than seeing, listening to, and dialoguing with the people you need to be responsible to. This dialogue should be a never-ending process that provides the input for design of new and improved products and services, new strategies, and new profit centers.

Creating Focus

To build the power of the river in your organization, you have to create focus. The focus on customers and on producing the results they need and want starts by deciding what customers you will commit yourself to serving.

This decision of what customers and what markets to serve is as important as what your product/service package will be. The strategic focus of Domino's Pizza was outlined when they decided to be in the "hot food at your door in minutes" business. But it became a commitment when they decided they would not serve people outside their stores' service areas.

Once they have selected which customers they will serve, great companies define clear strategies, goals, and objectives that reflect their commitment to those customers and how they will deliver the value in product and service that will excite them.

The strategies define the direction. The alignment of the organization's structure, systems, processes, and culture with those strategies builds power and efficiency. An organization's structure, systems, and processes should be designed so that it is easy for the customer to deal with the organization. Unfortunately, many organizations are designed to make it easy only for the people working there to do their jobs.

When strategy is in sync with market needs, the organization does not have to fight the marketplace. When the key strategic elements of structure, information and control systems, reward and recognition systems, and culture are in sync, the organization does not have to fight itself.

With this organizational architecture in place, all you need do is unleash the power of responsible people and your river will begin to flow with force.

Empowering Employees

Once we realized that managing the moments of truth was a key to service, we also realized that most moments of truth take place well out of sight of senior executives, managers, and supervisors. The answer to managing the moments of truth appears to be simple: Give people the authority they need to handle the jobs we give them.

Many organizations are now "empowering" their workforce, but we are learning that empowerment is really not that simple. It takes preparation, hard work, and follow-through.[9]

If you don't empower responsible, skilled, aligned, and informed people, it's like putting the inmates in charge of the asylum. What are these four attributes exactly? Let's look:

1. *Responsible:* Responsible workers and managers are responsible to the customer and to the organization, and they take responsibility for producing the results the customers want and the organization needs.

2. *Skilled:* People must have skills to be able to respond to the challenges they are given. The key skills include those needed to do the job, but they also include judgment and problem-solving ability, which enable people to take situations that aren't working and turn them into ones that are. To be effective in exercising responsibility, people need to be results-oriented problem solvers.

3. *Aligned:* Vision, mission, goals, and strategies provide the context for empowerment. They make it possible for creative, talented people to stay within the boundaries while making their own contribution to the success of the organization. When leaders and all of their colleagues are aligned in their vision, mission, goals, and strategies, empowerment works. When they aren't, it doesn't.

4. *Informed:* Too many theoretically empowered workers are operating without the power of information and without the opportunity to become better at what they are asked to do. If we are asking people to make the decisions that will ensure that customer and organizational needs are met, we have to give them the information they need to make those decisions. We also have to give them the information they need to know whether what they are doing is working or not, and whether they should keep up the work or make improvements fast.

Guided by the commitment to produce results that customers want, directed by a clear understanding of what those results are, and supported by well-defined strategies and a strategically aligned organization, responsible managers and workers take charge. It is time to get out of their way.

Notes

1. Jan Carlzon, *Moments of Truth* (New York: Perennial Library, 1989).
2. Karl Albrecht and Ron Zemke, *Service America* (Homewood, Ill.: Dow Jones-Irwin, 1985).
3. Tony Allesandra, Phil Wexler, and Rick Barrera, *Non-Manipulative Selling* (New York: Simon and Schuster, 1987).
4. Kenneth Blanchard and Sheldon Bowles, *Raving Fans: A Revolutionary Approach to Customer Service* (New York: Morrow, 1993).
5. Jan Carlzon, *Moments of Truth*.
6. Rick Barrera, *The Dollars and Sense of Exceptional Service Delivery* (San Diego: Rick Barrera and Associates, 1994).
7. Karl Albrecht and Ron Zemke, *Service America*.
8. Karl Albrecht, *The Only Thing That Matters* (New York: Harper Business, 1992).
9. Kenneth Blanchard, John P. Carlos, and Alan Randolph, *Empowerment Takes More Than a Minute* (San Francisco: Berrett-Koehler Publishers, 1996).

3

Developing Responsibility to the Organization

When we consider developing responsibility to the organization, we should focus on four major areas:

1. Creating an organization people would choose to be responsible to
2. Developing an understanding of the results organizations must achieve to be successful and what each individual can do to affect those results
3. Creating reward and recognition systems that are consistent with organizational goals and strategies
4. Developing an organization of results-oriented problem solvers

This chapter examines these four areas, focusing particularly on the first.

Creating an Organization People Would Choose to Be Responsible to

Developing responsibility to the organization starts with a simple question: What characteristics of an organization would cause you to choose to be responsible or committed to it? We've asked this question of hundreds of people in different companies and in different positions. Their answers have been surprisingly similar.

People would choose to be responsible to an organization that:

- Has a clear, meaningful sense of direction
- Has (and lives by) values they can respect
- Respects them and their contributions
- Has a compatible culture
- Is a source of pride
- Enables them to do challenging and meaningful work

We have conducted diagnoses of more than 3,000 organizations to assess their strategic architecture (vision, strategy, structure, information feedback and control systems, reward systems); their culture and functional areas (marketing and sales operations and human resources and financial systems); and a variety of key outcomes (revenue, profit, community image, morale, etc.). These diagnoses regularly reveal problems in the six key areas above in companies where responsibility is rated low.

Creating a Clear, Meaningful Sense of Direction

People want to know where they are heading. A clear understanding of the organization's vision, mission, goals, and strategy not only gives people comfort; it lets them share in the excitement of the journey. It gives them a context for their own decisions and lets them be creative contributors. Within this framework, employees can contribute their own solutions and use their own common sense, experience, skills, and judgment. And they can take pride in their contributions.

Individual responsibility is critical in the modern workplace. So is communicating a sense of direction and the focus and boundaries for desirable performance. This communication requires a variety of direction-setting tools to translate and cascade the vision of leaders into meaningful guidelines for everyone down the line and throughout the organization. The tools generally include:

- A clear statement of purpose and core values
- An inspiring and specific vision of an exciting future
- A clear statement reflecting the business we are in and how we are positioned in the marketplace
- A focused set of strategic initiatives that will lead us toward our vision in the shorter term (for example, one to three years)
- Processes and documents that communicate the vision, strategies, and goals and translate them into meaningful, concrete terms for those who will make them happen

All these tools involve both documents and processes that help us to develop and communicate their full meaning. And all these processes and documents should have one common element: They should all require the organization to stretch. They do not set an easy course but provide a real challenge to those who sign on for the journey.

Vision Statements

World leaders have long provided vision and inspiration to their people. Winston Churchill challenged his nation by demanding blood, sweat, and tears, and his people rose to the challenge in a heroic effort. Gandhi, David Ben-Gurion, Golda Meir, Anwar Sadat, Jack Kennedy, and Martin Luther King, Jr., all rallied their people to great human causes. Great business leaders also inspire their people with the power of their vision. Think back to Theodore Vale at AT&T, Alfred Sloan at GM, Tom Watson at IBM, Steve Jobs at Apple, and Jack Welsh at GE. If you are to lead, you must have a vision, and you must be able to see and convey that vision.

Those who do not understand the power of vision generally lose. Their message lacks power, hope, and excitement. In a speech in San Diego in the middle of his 1992 campaign for the presidency, George Bush said, "I just don't get the vision thing." It was obvious he didn't. For all his strength of character and talent as a statesman, Bush could not make his message resonate. It lay flat like a puddle when the people wanted the power of a river.

A vision statement is critical if you want to turn your organization into a powerful—and responsible—river. To be effective, it must provide the pull of a clear vision of a collective destiny and the focusing power of a solid purpose and a set of core values that will guide us as we seek that destiny.

The vision statement answers three questions:

1. Where are we going?
   - Answered by the vivid description of a desirable future and one or two challenging long-term goals
2. Why are we doing this?
   - Answered by a clear statement of our core purpose
3. Who are we?
   - Answered by a statement of our core values

To create a great vision, you have to look both forward and inward. Look forward to create a clear, vivid picture of a future you would be willing to work hard to produce. Look inward to identify what you are made of, what matters, and why you want to take the journey.

Unfortunately, for many people—leaders included—the day-to-day battles are often overwhelming or at least all-consuming. We get so focused on today that we can't see the vision of tomorrow. And we get so into *doing* that we stop *thinking*. But one critical role of leaders is to have that vision of the future always in mind and to share it, especially when others are losing sight of it in the details of everyday work.

Building a vision starts outside your organization by gathering perspective, looking at what others are doing, and listening to what others are saying. It builds with an in-depth understanding of your customers. The process includes looking into the future, anticipating changes in the world you must operate in. This often involves discussions with others who are planning their journeys so you have the chance to kick around your ideas. But most of all, creating a vision involves taking a long, creative look into the future and at the purpose and values that will provide the basis for the coming journey.

To prepare for the vision quest you have to get away from today. Put down the phone, walk away from the nagging problems. Go somewhere where you can relax and feel inspired. There, you can begin the search for the core purpose and values that underlie the organization and that will guide and inspire it as it strives to achieve both its long-term and day-to-day goals and objectives.

Next, take a mental journey into your future. Mentally visit the organization you would like to have in five or six years. Visualize yourself walking into the building, attending a staff meeting, interviewing a few customers, looking at the financials, and so on. Imagine examining the results the organization is producing. You want them to be exciting (remember, this is the future you want to have). Consider results in the three key areas of responsibility: customers, organizations, and people. These results of your desired future become meaningful goals in the present. When you have completed your mental journey, write down what you saw. This will form the future view of an exciting vision statement. Certainly it can be refined, edited and added to, but this gives you a place to start.

The Aspen Skiing Company believes its purpose is to provide the opportunity for renewal of the human spirit. This is very consistent with the purpose envisioned by Walter Paepcke, one of its original founders. Paepcke envisioned a community that would be the setting for a new Renaissance, a place that would bring together writers, scientists, artists, and businesspeople. To further this, Paepcke launched the Goethe Bicentennial Celebration in 1948 and the Aspen Institute for Humanistic Studies the next year.[1] The renewal of the spirit comes in many forms and will probably take the Aspen Skiing Company into many new and exciting directions in the years to come, even while it strives to maintain its image as the world's best ski area.

The most powerful visions create companies that last for decades. In one study James Collins and Jerry Porras showed that twenty visionary businesses outperformed the stock market by over twelve times over a multidecade period.[2]

Similarly, it was the Walt Disney Company's purpose to make people happy that led to Disneyland and the Epcot Center and the Anaheim Mighty Ducks. How much less would we have today if that early animator had thought his purpose was only to make cartoons?

Generally, strong vision statements come from strong leaders. They are often the work of one entrepreneurial or inspired person. This is certainly true in the early days of entrepreneurial companies and in later years for most companies. Strong visions reflect and articulate who the leader really is. They are not derived from analyzing the market. They are not tempered by practicality.[3]

The process of creating vision statements for start-up or young organizations can be different from that used to reenergize or refocus older, more mature organizations. In younger organizations the process is generally a one-person effort and is an attempt to give form to dreams and beliefs. There is little past or present to build on or learn from, and the vision may evolve over time. It becomes more like strategy in that, as the organization discovers its way, the vision changes until the right formula is found. Then it stabilizes and becomes the consistent base on which long-term success can be built.

With mature organizations, the effort is more often the work of a new leader or is a team event. The new leader or team searches the company past and present for the successful and powerful patterns as well as their own dreams and beliefs. Many companies are making this a team event. But we have found that this kind of team must be small, generally five to seven people, and they must be people with a feeling for the business and a high level of credibility with their colleagues.

Mission Statement

The term *mission* or *mission statement* has been used to describe so many different things that its meaning has become blurred. What people call mission statements today come in various forms. Some look a lot like vision statements, some are slogans that capsulize the essence of an organization, and others are a set of strategic (or not-so-strategic) goals. The critical complement to the vision statement is a positioning statement. It describes the organization in terms of the markets and needs it serves and the capabilities or unique strengths it brings to the marketplace. We call this positioning statement a market product scope (MPS) statement. It lets people know what business you're in and what you do that differentiates you from your competition. It helps people decide what to do and what not to do. It's created in response to market needs, competitive opportunities, and capabilities of your business.

The MPS statement can describe the business you have today, but it's more helpful if it describes what you want it to be tomorrow. In this way it sets the focus, mission, and need for stretch of the organization. Taken together, the market product scope statement and the strategic initiatives define the mission of the organization.

The market product scope statement should not stand alone. It should always be accompanied by a set of strategic initiatives that mark the journey from today's MPS statement to tomorrow's. All too often, leaders create vision and mission statements that proclaim a future that no one really believes in, is committed to, or is working on. Without the strategic initiatives—and, in fact, without operational plans and day-to-day effort—the dreams of leaders float above the workers like some cynical cloud.

This definition of a mission statement has a more stable element (the positioning or MPS statement) and a more adaptive element (the strategic initiatives). It needs to be visited regularly, usually annually, primarily to review and reconfirm the MPS and to redirect the organization through the strategic initiatives. The mission statement provides critical input—the boundaries—for operational or unit-level planning. The integration of all these elements is illustrated in Figure 3-1.

Operational Plans

Operational planning is a process of translation, diagnosis, and commitment:

• *Translation* of the organization's mission and strategies into unit missions, sets of strategic initiatives, and action plans that are consistent with the organization's vision, mission, and strategies and that are sufficiently clear to define the unit's assignment for the coming year.

Figure 3-1. The processes and products that provide a long-term vision linked to daily goals, objectives, and strategies.

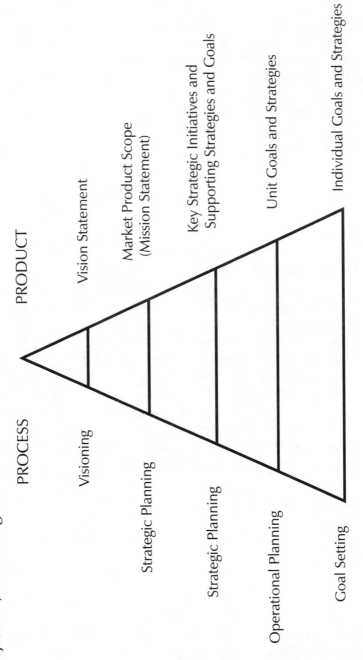

PROCESS   PRODUCT

Visioning   Vision Statement

Strategic Planning   Market Product Scope
                                   (Mission Statement)

Strategic Planning   Key Strategic Initiatives and
                                   Supporting Strategies and Goals

Operational Planning   Unit Goals and Strategies

Goal Setting   Individual Goals and Strategies

- *Diagnosis* of the unit's strengths and weaknesses relative to its assignment so that one can define what it needs to be able to deliver on that assignment.

- *Commitment* by unit leaders to an assignment from their leader.

An example of an operational planning process is shown in Figure 3-2.

Notice that Figure 3-2 has introduced a subtle shift in terminology. The key words are *assignment* and *accountability*. With the operational plans, we have moved into the realm of accountability. This is an organizational phenomenon, whereas responsibility is a personal phenomenon. Accountability happens in organizations when assignments are given by one person to another. With the assignment comes trust that the person chosen will deliver on the assignment. The challenge for managers is that they often do not directly control all that is needed to deliver on the assignment; yet they are held accountable for the results of others. This challenge to management is illustrated in Figure 3-3.

Operational planning starts with the delivery of an organizationwide planning document (that is, mission statement/strategic plan). The unit leaders review this document and identify which parts of it set the challenge for their unit. They then create a set of strategies, goals, and action plans that represents their unit's contribution to achieving the company mission.

When the top leaders receive the plans (commitments) from their people, they review them, negotiate any needed changes, and return the agreed-upon document to the unit leaders. This document then becomes the assignment they will be held accountable for.

Later, based on the budgeting process, units plan the resources they need to achieve the assignment. The budget goes through a similar iterative process. The budget further clarifies and reinforces the assignment and tests the strategy and plans to ensure that they provide adequate value to the organization for the costs incurred.

When working with clients in Australia, Gerry Faust devel-

Figure 3-2. The process of creating involvement, responsibility, and accountability in organizational planning.

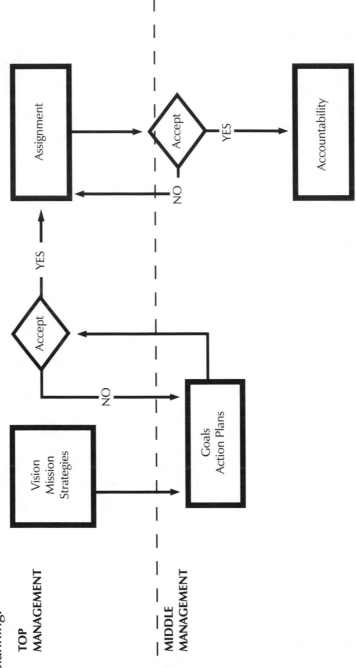

Figure 3-3. Assignments received by managers from executives and the consequent accountability of the managers for their workers' results.

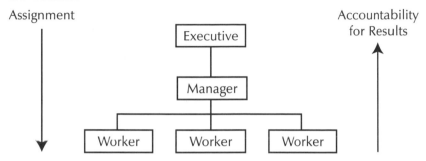

oped a short, simple exercise that helped to focus operational planning. He handed division directors the corporate strategic plan and asked them to highlight the words or phrases (the goals) that their divisions would have to achieve. Once they had finished the task, he said, "Now create a document that outlines the action plans (who will do what, by when, and how) you will commit to as your part of delivering on each word or phrase you highlighted." He also suggested that they might want to work with their team to verify the highlighting and to develop the action plans.

The highlighted corporate strategy documents were returned to the executive team with action plans attached. The executive team then evaluated whether the action plans from all divisions relative to a given word, phrase, or strategic initiative were sufficient to ensure success. If not, more planning had to be done. The executive team also identified elements of the strategy that had received no commitments. Gerry pointed out that these orphan elements could lead to only one of four interpretations:

1. They were "fluff" and ought to be eliminated.
2. These were assignments for the president or board of directors.
3. Someone had better be found to take them on.
4. Divine providence or luck was being relied on for these.

This exercise and related processes have been elaborated on and are now part of a team-based operational planning process we regularly use to ensure that strategic and operational plans are truly integrated. The key to success of the integrated planning processes (Figure 3-1) is that all elements are consistent and aligned with one another. From top to bottom, one should flow from another. From bottom to top, one should ensure the success of another.

At each level there needs to be general direction and specific guidance that is understandable to those who must deliver on the tasks assigned them. The only difference is that things generally get more concrete and shorter in term as we proceed down the organization. The CEO's vision may cover a five- to ten-year period, while a division director's may cover a three- to five-year period and a departmental manager's a one- to two-year period.

Here are some other key elements for effective planning:

• *The process is critical.* It should involve people and encourage the productive disagreement and questioning that are essential if you are to create plans that are better than any one person alone can create. The process itself should reflect and reinforce the culture you want in your organization.

• *You can have more than one document as an output from any planning process.* First create a document that is clear, understood, and agreed to by the participants in the process. Then create communications pieces (versions) for different audiences. Don't worry about other audiences during the creation; documents for them can be produced later. All too often, planners leave things vague or say things differently because of a specific audience they are worried about. Get the right concept and document first, then produce the communications pieces.

• *Plans should represent a stretch.* They should involve uncertainty but also possibility. They should provide the guidance and boundaries for creative, empowered people that allow them to exercise their abilities and still deliver on their assignments.

• *Plans are only plans, but implementation produces results.* Many plans do not affect results or activities as much as we would like them to. If we do not change what we are doing now, there will never be time to take on the new things. Strategic and operational planning necessitates letting go of old activities and methods to make room for the new. Leaders, managers, supervisors, and workers have to be prepared to live by new priorities and to decide what they will cease to do if they expect to implement new strategies. Focused efforts to get everyone to address this issue, to set new priorities, and to agree on what they will let go of are generally the best thing you can do to ensure the success of great new plans.

Having and Living by Values People Respect

Core values may drive a company's strategy and decisions and may be major determiners of its success. But they are not the only values companies are judged by. There are a number of other values, real or imagined, long-term or short-term, that affect whether people will choose to be responsible to a given organization.

Most people believe that a person's or a company's behavior is in some way reflective of their values. Human beings have a strong tendency to read intent into behavior.

As unproductive as it is to make assumptions about values or intentions, people do it anyway. Employees regularly infer the values of an organization from its behavior, and the values they infer would shock most of those businesses' leaders.

> One excitable entrepreneur has a hard time containing herself in a discussion. When she gets excited about an idea, she blurts it out, often while someone else is talking. Members of her executive team have lots of praise for her intellect, insight, and charisma. However, they also say, "She doesn't really value what we have to say" because of her "butting in." Of course, her behavior is a problem, but their diagnosis of the cause is incorrect.
>
> The entrepreneur was taught some group process skills and given some rules (for example, talk one at a time). Now she doesn't butt in, and because she acts as if she cares for and respects the input of her colleagues, they think she does.

As part of strategic planning processes, we regularly ask people to clarify their values and make active decisions about which values they want to keep and which they want to drop or change. This includes the core values that drive strategy as well as other values that people believe drive day-to-day decisions and behavior.

Once the values are defined and agreed on, you can talk about what behavior supports or detracts from those values. Responsible managers can then reflect on their own behavior and begin to work on doing things that are consistent with the values the team has agreed are important.

At American Fidelity, a successful midsize insurance company, senior managers worked to define the values and culture they wanted. They developed personal action plans that were commitments to actions that supported the agreed-upon desired values of the new culture. The plans were designed to require a personal stretch. The executives started with small commitments, but over time they became more dramatic. Probably the most courageous commitment and the biggest stretch came when the president and CEO of the company promoted several managers of subsidiaries to the title of president in one day, a title only he had held in the company for many years. He also delegated more authority and reduced his level of control, all in support of a statement that announced "We value initiative and responsibility in our empowered workforce."

All too often, companies espouse values but give little behavioral evidence that they exist. This really doesn't fool anyone. Workers are much more apt to believe what you do than what you say if the two are inconsistent. When you live the values and the culture, you will have no problem finding people who will choose to be responsible to your organization.

Respecting People and Their Contributions

People want to work in environments where they and their contributions are respected. When there is no respect, each day is demeaning. There is little sense of self-worth and contribution. Confident, optimistic, capable people will not stay in an environment that offers little respect.

If people work together in challenging environments, and particularly when they do so in a way that lets them experience the contributions of their colleagues, respect generally grows. Most people have valuable skills, talents, and insights. Most are prepared to do more under the right circumstances. Unfortunately, much of our workaday world does not let us see the real potential of our colleagues. This is probably one of the reasons why "adventure" or "challenge" training can have such a positive impact on teamwork. These activities bring people close together in challenging situations with focused objectives. Away from the constraints of the workplace and the stigma of job descriptions and titles, you see your colleagues in a new light. Most are able to earn respect in these situations.

The team-building theory behind the challenge courses and adventure outings is pretty straightforward. You put people in a situation that is difficult, preferably personally frightening, and where there is a common and challenging goal. Let these people face the fear together, work together, and accomplish the objectives together, and they will be a closer, better team after the experience.

You can create similar team-building experiences with similar characteristics in the workplace. Taking on tough problems that all agree are important and working together to solve them replicates most of the elements of challenge activities. Where does the fear come in? Work on an important and difficult problem that has been around for some time, probably because it has some scary element to it. For instance, you might have to challenge an old product line that was developed by the president's father or question a policy that the company has had for years. To get great solutions to difficult problems requires listening and learning and resolving differences of opinion. It requires teamwork.

Allowing people to participate in or even to play a key role in important things is the sincerest sign of respect. Calling them by their first name, listening to what they have to say, and letting them challenge your ideas or the status quo are also signs of respect. Properly run (see Chapter 11), problem-solving or process improvement teams can do more to create feelings of respect than almost anything else you can do.

In general, respect is fostered by participation, empowerment, and recognition. We've discussed participation and empowerment in Chapters 1 and 2, so let's focus for a moment on
recognition.

Recognition or acknowledgment is one of the great motiva-
tors. It can come in the form of "one minute praisings" and "one
minute reprimands."[4] It can come in the form of awards at ceremonies, even if the ceremony is only a five-minute pause on the
production line. Sometimes it's just stopping to share your perspective or a suggestion on how to do things better. The key to
recognition is that it be honest.

A little eye contact, a friendly smile, a stop to chat—any one
of these can be a form of recognition. And the higher up the
corporate ladder you are, the more your personal time and acknowledgment are valued as recognition and reinforcement.

Tom Monaghan, founder of Domino's Pizza, was a great
recognizer. At every management meeting, he would ask the
vice presidents for reports on who was doing great things. If he
heard something he really liked, he'd go out after the meeting
to congratulate and shake the hand of one of the people he had
just heard about. The handshake was usually followed by a personal gift. In the early days it was a monogrammed tie. Later it
became a watch with the employee's initials on it.

There are actually two systems at work in building respect
and providing recognition: the formal system, and the personal
or informal system. Almost all that we've discussed so far deals
with the informal system. The formal system—including formal
compensation, recognition, and incentive systems—also has its
impact. To the degree that the formal system is fair and functional, it can be a great tool for building respect. It cannot replace
the informal methods, but it can reinforce or negate them. We
will say more about formal recognition and rewards later in this
chapter.

Having a Compatible Culture

The culture of an organization is the embodiment of its true values and philosophy. It is expressed in the typical behavior of its

employees and in its policies, procedures, systems, structures, decisions, and day-to-day actions. The culture of an organization is much like its personality. A company can be described in personality terms (as, for example, "a happy, fun, and caring place").

To the degree that your personality is consistent with the culture of an organization you are likely to feel comfortable. Driven people with personalities that focus on results like companies with similar cultures. People with personalities that focus on process and systems are more at home in companies with similarly oriented cultures.

As organizations grow and develop, their cultures change. Start-ups may be heavily oriented toward entrepreneurship but soon focus on producing results as they strive to make ends meet. They may then get more entrepreneurial again and move into an expansive rapid growth stage. With these changes come challenges. A company whose culture matched someone's personality at one time can evolve to having a different culture that may be less comfortable for that individual. Dramatic culture changes can occur with acquisitions or other important events. Small entrepreneurial companies acquired by megacorporations for their innovation and growth potential are often traumatized by the new, more bureaucratic cultures they must contend with. In these cases, the entrepreneurial leaders and many of their similarly inclined colleagues tend to jump ship as soon as they can. Why? The personality/culture conflict is too much to tolerate.

There are other aspects of culture, and, in fact, culture and values are generally very much intertwined. However, in both these areas the critical factor is the alignment of personal beliefs, values, standards, and personalities with those of the organization. The greater the alignment is, the easier it is for people to choose to be responsible to the organization.

Being a Source of Pride

Pride is a powerful motivator. People like to take pride in their organization. It can come from the company's environmental or community programs, its growth, its size, its profits, its leader, its product or services, or from any number of other sources.

Recently, a company president came to us to discuss his organization. He complained that motivation was low throughout and wondered what he could do about it. Almost in unison, we said, "Do the things that will make the company successful." This was not the most helpful answer. He would have to create increased commitment, motivation, and responsibility before the company would achieve success. However, motivation is low in most failing organizations, and it is high in most truly successful organizations. Motivation increases naturally as people see their organization doing the things they believe will make it more successful.

Pride is a personal thing. What turns one person on could theoretically turn another off. Like most of the other factors mentioned in this section, pride is somewhat self-selecting. That is, the people who choose to stay are the ones who can take pride in what the organization is or does. Those who can't will eventually leave, which is good because people who stay and don't have pride in the organization will not generally choose to be responsible to it and will therefore not be high-level contributors to its ultimate success.

The message to leaders is simple. Consider how you can build pride in the organization. Do it in different ways. Celebrate and communicate the victories and tell the stories of your successes. Listen and learn from the people. Find out what they are most proud of, and then do more of it. But most of all, build a successful organization. That will motivate everyone.

Enabling People to Do Challenging and Meaningful Work

The greatest motivator in the workplace is challenging, meaningful work. It has the greatest potential to make people feel good about themselves and the organization they work for. To provide this fulfillment, the work must be worth doing. Doing it well must be an accomplishment. The work should require stretch and have some level of uncertainty in which the judgment, problem solving, or decision making of the worker can make a difference.

These criteria do not mean that manual labor is less motivating than knowledge work. For example, in a recent session of interior landscapers from Nordstrom, an excited young woman spoke about how beautiful her flowers made the open spaces in the store. She told how a woman passing by had commented on the flowers as she was putting in the new selection. She gave the woman a big smile and handed her two of the pots of petunias she was removing. Then she added, "I told her, 'You take these. We'll only throw them away and I know you'll give them a good home.'" Here was a worker who was excited about her challenging and meaningful work. She was making it that way by her own creativity, judgment, and decisions. And she was certainly creating moments of magic for Nordstrom customers.

Developing Understanding of the Results Organizations Must Have to Be Successful

To be truly successful, a business needs to produce results for customers, owners, and employees. We like to say you have to provide great service, generate great business results, and be a great place for responsible people to work. These are the three key results areas for businesses and represent the triple bottom line for successful companies. They are intimately tied to one another, and success in any one over the long term is tied to success in the others. Fail in any one, and over time you will fail altogether.

Organizations that wish to succeed over time understand these results and evaluate themselves regularly in all these areas. Chapter 2 focused on the first of these areas. In the first part of this chapter we discussed many of the key factors in the third of these areas. Now we'll turn to how to give people the knowledge and skills they need to help build a great business.

Well-run organizations must produce the desired results while making effective use of their resources. For businesses, this means they must produce profits, cash, and value. Many of the tough decisions that management must make relate to the balance, trade-offs, and timing among these three areas. One of the major challenges of business leaders is teaching more of their people the complex interrelation among these three factors, how the company moves these numbers, and how what they do contributes to moving them. With this knowledge, people have the opportunity to act responsibly to the whole business and to work for results that count.

Traditionally, these numbers and the things that affect them have been the secret domain of owners and senior managers. Today, many are trying to take the mystery out of the numbers. By teaching more and more people how businesses work, business leaders are finding that they are developing new, more effective partners in the battle to improve the numbers. But you can't just teach people accounting if you want this approach to work. You have to give them the big picture of how businesses interact with the outside world of competitors, suppliers, customers, investors, and bankers. You have to teach them the intricacies of the total system of a business. Only when people understand the context of the business and of the decisions they make are they truly armed to be fully responsible. Only then are they ready to learn about and to go to work on the numbers.

If you combine this form of business literacy with the proper measurements, regular review of the measurements, and focused problem solving, you have a great formula for success. The approach to teaching people about business requires practice and application. They must actually play the game of business to get better at it.

Providing Information on Key Organizational Success Factors

It has been said that if you want something to change, measure it. Part of the reason for this is the emphasis that is created by the measurement and the focus it puts on a single variable. When Bob Crandal, CEO of AMR, the parent company of American Airlines, wanted baggage-handling performance to improve, he simply asked for a monthly baggage report that came directly to him. A little command emphasis goes a long way toward focusing people's minds.

However, the value of measuring is not just one of emphasis. Measuring—particularly comparing planned or desired performance with actual performance—points to the gaps and sets the stage for problem solving. We use review and action planning (RAP)[5] meetings as the mechanism for reviewing the information, identifying the gaps, and launching appropriate problem-solving efforts.

The RAP meeting is held after everyone has had a chance to review his numbers, often with his team. Each senior manager says a few words about his activities and successes during the past month and then identifies his three most important deviations from plan (gaps). The term *plan* means more than just budgets. It includes things like desirable delivery times and when a piece of equipment should be installed. RAP participants explain the reason *why* the gap is important, what they propose to do about it, the help they will need, or if they want to put the gap on the table for some team-based analysis and problem solving.

There is some dialogue if there are other opinions about the key gaps or suggestions regarding the proposed action plans. Problem solving is postponed until the problem-solving part of the meeting or may be assigned to an off-line team.

The objective of the RAP meeting is to quickly identify problems and to focus problem solving on important areas. Problem solving can start only after problems are recognized. So everything that helps people to clearly understand goals (desired results), and helps people to identify the gaps between goals and actual results, facilitates problem solving.

The RAP meeting is designed to enhance personal and team responsibility. Its agenda and process are based on a number of the principles discussed throughout this book; it is designed to create a productive learning environment, reinforce responsibility, build teamwork, and increase business literacy. It focuses on results and identifying problems that need to be solved.

The Need for Information, Not Just Data

Data collection is one area where more may not be better. That is, too much information may actually make it harder to identify "meaningful gaps." The process of selecting the key indicators of success in any area of business is an important one for those who manage. Getting reports down to a single page of key indicators with comparisons of desired and actual results helps keep everyone from losing sight of the important owing to the volume of the irrelevant. This helps ensure that what you review is important, usable information, not just reams of irrelevant data.

If you take almost any key success indicator, work to understand what could have an impact on that number, and then stretch your thinking, you can figure out ways to make that number move. This is especially true if you use a team of people from different departments. The approach that goes the furthest to involve people in the financial results of an organization is open-book management. This approach generally has four key elements:

1. Building business literacy
2. Opening the books
3. Empowering people to act
4. Sharing the gains

This approach begins with training in how and why business works, and it follows with in-depth instruction on the numbers that affect profits, equity, and the generation of cash. There is also analysis to set performance baselines. A critical characteristic of every open-book approach is teamwork. With this as their base, teams work, generally from the grass roots up, to regularly evaluate progress and create improvements.

Typically, these programs take years to fully implement and involve performance-based bonus programs and most of the sound business principles we've discussed thus far. Sound market and customer analysis, a deep understanding of purpose and core values, a clear vision, mission, and strategies are all essential to effective open-book management.

Open-book management is not for everyone, although it is growing in acceptance. It requires great preparation and a huge commitment to the development of people. But, in many cases, the results are impressive.

Rewarding and Recognizing the Performers

The objective of reward and recognition programs should be to motivate and sustain high levels of performance. Technically, this can be done intrinsically or extrinsically. Intrinsic motivation derives from the challenge, meaning, or joy of the work. The early parts of this chapter focused on things you can do to make the work more challenging, meaningful, exciting, and fun. In this section, the focus is more on the extrinsic incentives of rewards (money, benefits, perks) and recognition. With all incentives, particularly rewards, the goal is to create win-win situations for the organizations and those who work in them. The people and the organization should be in the same boat so that if the organization wins, the people win. This can be done through total compensation programs or with incentive elements that overlay basic pay and benefit programs. Compensation systems, in general, should be set up to reward performance over time and to aid in the retention and development of high performers. However, basic compensation systems are not the focus of this section. Rather, we focus on some of the key considerations for those who would use recognition and variable rewards as a method of motivating people to higher levels of performance.

Incentives and variable pay appear to be getting more popular. There is, however, a real danger that overeager executives will attempt to overcome the built-in challenges to their organization the easy way: by providing great incentives rather than doing the hard work of creating more broad-based organizational change. Performance-based incentive programs are not intended to be a panacea. They are not intended to and won't work to overcome poor products, services, positioning, strategies, promotion, distribution, or location.

Here are some suggestions for designing reward and recognition programs that reinforce strong performance and motivate excellence:

• *Design incentive systems as the final and capstone step in achieving strategic alignment.* Briefly, here are the steps of this alignment process. First, set the vision, values, mission, and strategy of the organization. Second, create an organizational structure with staffing and delegation appropriate to assigned responsibilities that facilitates achievement of the strategy. Next, establish information, monitoring, and control systems. These provide the information people need to make the decisions they must make to accomplish the strategy and improve results. Then, establish the system for allocating (budgeting) resources to support the structure and the plan. Finally, when all these things are working, consider broad performance-based incentive systems.

Without the previous work, people will be offered incentives that give them little or no control over their fate. People working under prematurely implemented, poorly planned performance-based pay systems are apt to become severely distressed, and their work will suffer.

• *Be careful that your incentive programs do not discourage behaviors you want.* For example, many sales programs provide incentives for getting new customers but not for keeping old customers. This short-term emphasis can hurt businesses (like insurance) in which there is a high cost of sale and in which significant customer retention is needed to recover those costs before a profit is made.

• *Don't put all your eggs in one "big system" basket.* Save some of your incentive dollars for special events, impromptu awards, or focusing attention on a particular variable for a short period. The problem with the big long-term systems is that things can change. What looked like a great idea at the beginning of the year may not seem so terrific in October.

• *Change the incentive system regularly so that it retains its motivational power.* Bonus systems that never change become part of the background and are taken for granted. Announce systems for one year, and review their value and the method of implementation before the year is up. Maintain enough flexibility to move with the real needs of the business and change the program once in a while to keep it exciting.

• *Match the complexity of the system with the knowledge of those who work within it.* In general, simpler is better. Don't base incentives on profits if your people don't understand how profits are made and what they can do to improve or erode them. A corollary to this is first provide the understanding, then provide the incentive system.

• *Combine companywide, individual, and team bonuses for maximum effect.* Remember, incentives are designed to produce a desired behavioral outcome. Individual incentives are more appropriate for some tasks, functions, and performances, for example, personal sales, while team incentives may be more appropriate for such activities as customer service and order fulfillment. Generally, the goal is to have some portion of the incentive tied to overall company performance. The important thing is not to reward individual or subunit performance unless it helps the organization. Also, make bonuses self-funding wherever possible. That is, pay them out of the profits made on that which is being rewarded.

• *Provide shorter-term measurements (that is, numbers reported in weekly or monthly meetings) and short-term or on-the-spot recognition of good performance to mitigate the negative effects of making people wait overly long for a payoff.* The longer the payoff is deferred, the more the other pressing day-to-day challenges will overcome the power of the incentive.

• *Put everyone—managers and workers alike—on similar bonus plans.* This helps build trust, mutual respect, and true teamwork. This should not negate the previous points. Rather, it is merely to say that the more we are in the same boat, the greater the collaboration and trust will be.

• *Plan for both bad and good months, quarters, and years.* Before you implement any system like this, you had better think: "What will happen if we have a very bad year? What should we do with a windfall profit that had nothing to do with the company's performance?" We believe in stacking the deck in favor of success when launching new incentive programs. But have a contingency plan in the event of poor performance.

Going with more conservative incentives at the beginning gives you a chance to test your system. Reserving some percentage of the monthly or quarterly bonus for the end of the year helps prevent problems when the last half of the year doesn't live up to the promise of the first half.

- *To be effective, make sure that the incentives you offer will make a difference in people's lives.* It takes considerable extra effort to make major changes in organizations, and the incentives have to be commensurate with that effort. Although there is no fixed rule, it appears that bonuses of approximately 10 percent of base pay are needed to make a major difference.

- *Remember that recognition is a great motivator.* Don't just focus on rewards. The reality is that bonuses have the desired effects only when a lot of other things are done incredibly well. Recognition can act as the more immediate reinforcer when you use monthly, quarterly, or annual bonuses. It is still a major driver for the vast majority of people and should not be over-looked in any program intended to motivate high levels of per-formance.

Developing a Team of Results-Oriented Problem Solvers

When people work for an organization they are ready to commit themselves to, know what results they must produce, have the requisite information, and have a proper reward and recognition system, the only challenge left is providing people with the skills and knowledge that will enable them to create the results. The basic skills are problem solving and decision making.

With this in mind, we focus for the remainder of the book on the critical role of judgment and problem solving in produc-ing results, and on providing some in-depth instruction in the artful science of solving problems with teams in organizations.

Notes

1. Peter Shelton, *Aspen Skiing—The First Fifty Years* (Telluride, Colo.: Western Eye Press, 1997).
2. James Collins and Jerry Porras, *Built to Last: Successful Habits of Visionary Companies* (New York: Harper Business, 1994).
3. Ibid., p. 65.

4. Kenneth Blanchard and Spencer Johnson, *The One Minute Manager* (New York: Berkley Books, 1981).
5. Dr. Gerald W. Faust and Will Phillips, *How to Turn Your Monthly Management Meeting into a RAP Session* (San Diego: Faust Management Corporation, 1990).

4

The Responsible Manager
as a Problem Solver

There are many reasons why organizations don't produce the results they desire. Here is a list of the reasons we have heard recently:

"We are in the wrong location."

"We are not positioned properly in the marketplace."

"Our suppliers are providing low-quality products."

"Our people aren't skilled at selling."

"Our competitors are lowering their prices."

"We don't get the information we need to make decisions."

Are these really reasons businesses don't produce the desired results, or are they just problems these organizations need to solve? We believe the answer is both. They are reasons organizations don't produce results *and* they are problems these organizations need to solve. Responsible managers don't use these reasons as excuses. They just get on with the problem solving. Problem solving plays a central role in responsible management. Responsible managers are results-oriented problem solvers. When results aren't happening, they start the problem solving.

A problem can be defined as a situation in which we are not

achieving desired results. Problems are generally of two types. The first type involves situations in which what we are doing does not create the desired result because there is a barrier between where we are and where we want to be. For example, I want to open a new store on the other side of town, but I don't have enough capital. The lack of capital is the barrier, the new store is what I want. The problem could be stated as "The lack of capital is keeping me from expanding into a critical new market."

The other problems are ones of process. That is, I am doing what I believe needs to be done, but I am not getting the results I want. For example, I have a sales program for a new product that is not producing the desired level of revenues. The sales program is what I am doing, higher sales are what I want. The problem may be stated as "The current sales program is not producing the desired level of sales."

The key to better results is removing barriers and improving or changing processes. It is all about solving problems. When you take responsibility for results, you soon realize that even if you do everything just as you were trained to, you still may not achieve the desired results. In such cases, the responsible manager doesn't merely throw up her hands and say, "Well, I tried my best," or, "I did what I was told." To the contrary, she steps back and tries something new. She analyzes the situation, engages her problem-solving skills, and renews her efforts to reach her goals.

But the problems of organizations are not often what we think they are. They are not just little things that go wrong. If they were, most people could fix them and the organizations would be back on track. Rather, they are multifaceted, multicaused phenomena that affect the organization in many ways over a long period of time. A recent experience dramatically illustrates this point.

Over thirty CEOs of midsize companies are gathered for a seminar. The speaker asks the CEOs to list five of the most meaningful problems affecting their companies. The group is then asked, "How many of you have lists where three or more of the problems have been problems for more than three months?" All the participants raise a hand. The question is repeated with different time frames: six months? one year? two years? At three years, almost all hands are still raised.

What is wrong with this picture?

- The problems identified were supposed to be important—the most meaningful ones.
- The respondents could identify the problems.
- The known problems had persisted for years.
- The respondents were the "leaders" of their companies.

This exercise has been repeated over and over again in seminars throughout the world. Always the result is the same. Problems aren't getting solved. Managers and leaders are getting frustrated.

Why Problems Don't Get Solved

If problems are the reason organizations aren't producing the results they need and want, and if results are so important, why aren't problems getting solved? This is an interesting question with a complex answer. For now, let's simplify the answer by focusing on some very specific reasons why problems don't get solved.

- Problems aren't identified.
- Problems aren't identified by the right people.
- Problems are avoided.
- People are too busy doing to think about solutions.
- People don't know how to solve problems.

Let's take a look at these challenges to learn more about what it takes to be a responsible manager.

Problems Aren't Identified

There is no doubt that some problems don't get solved because no one sees them as problems. This is often the result of focusing on activities rather than on results or some misunderstanding as to what the results are supposed to be. For instance, there's the receptionist who believes that her job is to answer the phone but who has no insight into the negative impact of her lackluster greeting. Or there's the trainer whose goal is to cover the content of his course rather than to help people really learn what they need to do to achieve success. He thinks the day went well when he gets through all the topics.

In these cases, the challenge is to provide people with a clear understanding of the important results their work is supposed to produce and to help them understand how they can make a contribution in creating these results. Only when people know the goal and can see the results of their work can they identify the gaps between what is desired and what is actually happening. Managers who want to focus on results must help people to see the difference between desired and actual performance.

Many problems aren't identified because identifying problems is culturally unacceptable in the organization. This is common in aging organizations where the mantra is "Everything is fine, don't make waves." It is reinforced by managers who don't like the word *problem* or who shoot the bearer of bad tidings. Anything that forces problems underground sets the stage for irresponsible management.

Another reason that problems are not identified is that some people are simply afraid to face them. Not identifying them is an easy way to avoid having to deal with them.

When the problems are under the table, in the dark, so to speak, they can be scary. But, when the light is on and the issues are on the table, when the problems are identified, we generally find that there is just some problem solving to be done. The more experience and success the organization has with problem solving, the more comfortable it feels in such situations. It might be difficult, it might take some work, but it is not so scary. Look at problems as potential opportunities for improvement. They indicate where the responsible manager can start to make a difference.

Leaders often have to be the ones who turn on the light. When Gil Amelio became president of the troubled National

Semi Conductor, he had his senior executives provide him with an overview of their areas. Each report he received was positive and upbeat. This was a company that was in real trouble. Amelio was incredulous that not one of these executives talked about problems. When they were done, he exclaimed, "Everyone tells me how well we're doing and we're bleeding to death. . . . Don't any of you have any problems?" The search for problems—and subsequently solutions—was the key to National Semi Conductor's turnaround.

Another CEO of a large construction company was so frustrated by his team's unwillingness to admit problems that he decided he had to do something dramatic. He started off his next management meeting by telling about his greatest screwup as a manager, one that had cost his company hundreds of thousands of dollars. When he was done, he emptied the $300 in his wallet onto the table and announced, "So tell me about the mistakes you've made. The one with the biggest screwup gets the pot."

All too often we are afraid of being wrong, of admitting mistakes or problems. But on the table, in the light, the mistakes become opportunities for improvement and targets for our problem-solving efforts.

Two activities that can be used to turn on the light are monthly review and action planning (RAP) meetings and an annual diagnosis. The RAP sessions were discussed in Chapter 3. They make it the responsibility of managers to identify problems in their area and to help focus problem solving on important problems that are impeding company strategies and progress toward goals.

The annual diagnosis is a major activity designed to provide strategic direction to the problem-solving process. All too often, problem solving is seen as tactical and reactive. We believe problem solving must be a strategic, ongoing process in organizations. It ought to be focused on the big issues and the high-value opportunities for improvement.

In its simplest form, diagnosis is intended to turn on the light. It asks the question "What are we doing now that we could do better?" A great diagnosis:

1. Involves many people in the process.
2. Makes it easy to bring all the issues into the light.

3. Focuses on identifying problems the company has some ability to solve and on working on causes, not symptoms.
4. Results in clear priorities and action plans being set.
5. Provides a baseline for evaluating progress over time.

We have developed several tools that fit these criteria. One is the Executive Insight™ process, which plays like a game. Designed for departments and smaller organizations (under 200 people), it involves five to ten leaders in sorting cards that present problems organizations commonly have. The cards are sorted into categories: those that are "clues" to the opportunities for change in this organization (that is, problems we have), and those that aren't.

The cards are all coded to indicate their cause-and-effect relationship to one another. We have found that organizational problems can be roughly divided into five groupings:

1. *External factors.* These are problems that are outside the control of the organization but that affect us, like government regulation or competitors. Some of these problems we can influence; others we just have to adapt to.
2. *Culture characteristics.* These reflect the way we are but may have a negative impact on us.
3. *Strategic problems with the strategic architecture of the company.* These include problems with purpose and direction, structure, information and control systems, and rewards and recognition systems.
4. *Functional elements of the organization.* These include problems in sales, marketing, customer service, operations, human resources, finance and accounting areas.
5. *Problems with key results.* These can include problems with productivity, revenues, profits, image in the community, and morale.

A general representation of the cause-and-effect model underlying the Executive Insight™ process is presented in Figure 4-1.

Clues in these categories are arranged in patterns, and the categories and their component patterns reveal the cause-and-

Figure 4-1.　Representation of the cause-and-effect model.

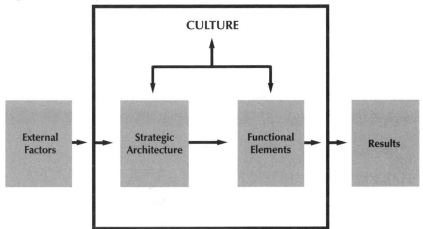

effect relationships between the clues. The external factors affect the company, including its culture and strategic and functional elements, which in turn combine to affect results. Culture is actually an effect and a cause. That is, a company is formed, its culture then emerges (an effect), and in turn it begins to affect what we decide, reward, and do (a cause).

The Executive Insight™ process helps leaders create a common understanding of their issues and their relation to one another. Then it takes them through a process of priority setting and action planning, which leads to consensus, provides focus to the problem-solving effort, and ensures that it is directed at high-value areas of potential improvement.

A similar model forms a base for the second diagnostic tool, a comprehensive computer-scored organizational diagnostic questionnaire. This questionnaire allows you to gather data from throughout the organization and to assess the total organization and its various parts. The statistics also permit the creation of a number of scores on factors that we believe affect an organization's ability to succeed over time.

You need not use these specific tools in your diagnosis. You can make a substantial contribution to the success of any organization by using any number of diagnostic processes. Some may be as simple as a two-day retreat at which you focus on bringing problems into the light, attempting to understand them, setting priorities, and creating commitment to focusing your corporate problem-solving energy on one or two key problems.

With this simple start, you begin to make problem solving a strategic process in your organization. Then, if you follow the guidelines in the next two chapters, you can make that problem solving even more productive.

Problems Aren't Identified by the Right People

There are times when problems do get identified—but by the wrong people. The wrong people are people who do not have what it takes to get the problems solved.

Recently, a friend tried an experiment. In his supposedly smart, empowered company, he held a "Boy, is that stupid" meeting. The meeting started out with some stories about how we often go on doing things that are stupid, and the importance of continuous improvement. He used enough humor so that people began having fun and started to loosen up. Then he popped the big question. "Is there anything you see in your area—or in anyone else's area—that you think is really stupid?" There was a long silence, then a receptionist very tentatively raised her hand and explained the stupid way that calendars were kept and updated. One after another, people began making observations, asking questions, and reaching decisions. Sometimes, what appeared to be stupid actually had a valid rationale, but in the course of two hours, eight critical changes were made and eight really stupid things stopped happening in that organization.

An organization is like a giant beach ball. Each person stands on that beach ball at some point. From any one person's position, you can see some of the ball, but not all of it. Only when we share our different perspectives can we understand the whole thing. And unfortunately, sometimes you see something wrong in your area that you don't have the ability to change. Getting authority to the people with the knowledge of the problems, or the knowledge to those with authority, is critical to making an organization truly responsible. However, authority is not all that is needed to solve a problem. Authority may provide the "legal" right to solve a problem, but it certainly does not ensure that a good solution will be developed.

There are really four things that have to be brought together in order to solve problems efficiently and effectively: (1) an understanding of the problem; (2) the authority to do something about it; (3) the appropriate knowledge or expertise to solve the problem; and (4) the power to ensure effective and efficient implementation of decisions. Responsible organizations install formal systems or processes that make it easy to identify problems, set priorities, and put the right people together with the right problems. These processes include activities at management and staff meetings, annual climate and organizational surveys, and more comprehensive organizational diagnoses.

Problems Are Avoided

A short fairy tale may be instructive in helping us understand why problems are sometimes avoided, even over long periods of time.

> Once upon a time, there was a very aggressive manager of a brick-making factory. He was very committed to solving problems in his factory. He carried two big guns at all times, and whenever he saw a problem he shot it.
>
> Most of his problems were trolls who ran through the factory and created havoc. But the manager regularly removed them, so things were going pretty well. He got a reputation as a great troll eliminator. Soon everyone was bringing him trolls, and he was dispatching them with ease.
>
> One day as he sat in his room with his guns on his desk, waiting for the next troll to be brought in, a strange thing happened. A huge dragon appeared in the doorway. The manager quickly took up his guns, but before he shot, he realized, "Shooting will only irritate the dragon. I need to do something else." He ran to the

door. "Pleased to meet you, sir," he said to the dragon. "Would you come with me? We have a nice area for dragons in the courtyard." And with that, the manager ushered the dragon into the courtyard. A few weeks later, the same thing happened, and another dragon was added to the courtyard.

As the years went by, the trolls were regularly eradicated, but the dragons in the courtyard multiplied, and one day the dragons ate the whole factory.

What is the meaning of this story? There are two important lessons to be learned here.

1. *Sometimes you need more than a gun to keep problems out of your factory.* It is very easy in these days of complex and deep organizations, involving many disciplines, departments, and responsibilities, to find problems that require more energy, authority, power, or expertise than any one person has. Sometimes the problems are like the proverbial Gordian knot. They appear so complex that they can't be solved by mere mortals. They involve many interrelationships and convoluted cause-effect elements. Each time you think of a solution you come up with another problem. Such problems are often avoided just because they seem too tough to solve.

2. *Sometimes we ignore problems because we don't want to deal with them.* How many organizations have dragons in the courtyard that they don't want to deal with? Difficult problems that are known to exist but that people just don't want to face? Often these are personnel problems, like the long-term employee who no longer is performing or the person who has been promoted to his level of incompetence. Sometimes these problems are almost institutionalized in the company. "We've always been in this business," said one manager, discussing the rationale for a product line that regularly resulted in a negative contribution to profit and overhead.

Sometimes dragons hang around because the people who do see them are afraid to point them out to the people with the big guns. As the CFO of a midsize company said recently, "I realize this is a problem, but the CEO doesn't like to hear about problems."

People Are Too Busy

Have you ever gone to work and "lost the day?" You went to the office with good intentions only to see the day disappear as you reacted to all that was going on there. Your life gets taken over by the fax machine, e-mail, and voice mail, or your day disappears as you respond to a vice president, your secretary, and the person who stands at your door clearing his throat until you look up.

What is the point of all this? It's simple. Most managers are doers. They want to make things happen, and often they get so into the doing of the apparently urgent that they lose sight of or don't get around to the truly important things. Doing becomes a habit.

Peter Drucker has said that management must be a balance between rowing and steering. The higher you are in the organization, the more you must steer. As we work our way up the corporate ladder, the necessary and rewarded skills change. Early on it is the rowing—the hard work, dedication, and doing—that brings the bonuses and the kudos. But somewhere in the middle management ranks, a subtle shift takes place, and the thinking, steering, leading, and coaching become the keys to further success.

You can't sufficiently identify problems, let alone solve them or create meaningful change, without taking a step back to see the forest as well as the trees. Too many problems remain unsolved because managers don't stop doing long enough to clearly identify them.

People Don't Know How to Solve Problems

Let's assume that a problem is identified by the right people. It is admitted, and they are ready and willing to take on the challenge; they are even ready to stop doing long enough to do what it takes to solve the problem. But still, the problem doesn't get solved because those who know of it and want to deal with it don't know how to solve problems.

In terms of skills, problem solving is the key to responsible organizations and responsible managers. All too often, eminently solvable problems go unsolved because people don't take the time to clearly define the problem, clarify the desired outcome, think out of the box, or carefully plan the implementation of an otherwise great solution. They don't take the time to find the flaws in their implementation plan, communicate the solution clearly so that others understand and support it, or manage the implementation of the solution they have created.

There are also good people who solve problems in ways that hurt teamwork, don't involve key people, create more problems than they solve, and so on.

The point of all this is simple. Some people are naturally good problem solvers. Some intuitive solutions end up being the best ones. Some aren't and some don't. Also, an organization's problems can be complex, and their solution shouldn't be left to chance. Finally, when an organization has a problem-solving method, when its people know how to use that method, big problems are a lot less scary and really do become opportunities.

In the following chapters we will focus on what it takes to become a great results-oriented problem solver and how you can use and lead teams that will create the results that will make you and your organization a winner in the great game of business.

5

A Problem-Solving
Approach That Works

With the exception of certain kinds of mechanical failure or equipment breakdown, no two problems are the same. Rarely, if ever, is a manager likely to encounter two decisions or problems that are identical. Contrary to the popular myth, history never repeats itself exactly.

However, there are different categories of problems with characteristic similarities. An understanding of these categories, and the commonalities of the problems within each category, can be of great benefit to the manager. The three basic categories of problems are:

1. *People*. These problems are caused primarily by the behavior of an individual or a group of people.

2. *Operational*. These problems are caused primarily by factors other than people or technology. These include such things as policy, organizational structure, and the dynamics of the marketplace or the economy, and involve problems in such functional specialties as finance, marketing, operations, and public relations.

3. *Technical*. These problems are caused primarily by mechanical, technical, electrical, electronic, or hydraulic equipment components and/or system functioning or failure to function.

In addition, three levels of variables shape the outcome of most events: (1) causal, (2) intervening, and (3) output.

Responsible managers search for causality when solving problems. This means that they seek to determine the primary or root cause of a particular effect or set of outcomes. Causal events are the triggering events, conditions, or phenomena that start the chain reactions which ultimately create a desired or undesired effect.

The intervening variables, also called shaping variables, are factors that arise at the intermediate points in the chain reaction which alter or shape the final effects or outcomes. Without the causal factors, these intervening factors likely would not make a difference. However, they do come into play as a result of the causal circumstances and affect these events in such a way as to shape the final outcome.

The final level is the output level. These are data or conditions of final effect. Often these variables are referred to as the symptoms or the consequences of the real cause. Analysis conducted at this level is end-results analysis and takes into account that this is the end of the chain. Attempts to solve problems by addressing only output variables usually result in solutions that are little more than window dressing. This is usually what has happened when the problem solvers are accused of dealing with the symptoms and not the cause.

In the space shuttle *Challenger* disaster, the causal factors were the faulty O-rings in the booster seals. Intervening variables include the response of the technicians to the information they had about the possible impact of the faulty seals on the operation of the boosters. Output variables include the various effects of the explosion on its surroundings and all the other results—human and technical—of the explosion.

Problems are determined to be people, operational, or technical in nature depending on the nature of the causal variables—not on the nature of factors that exist at either the intervening or the output level. Many disasters occur because problem solvers focus on the intervening or output level rather than on the causal level to determine how a problem should be dealt with. Consider the following example.

A CEO assigns the responsibility for completing a study of inventory policy and procedures to a mid-level manager. The CEO tells the manager to get help from whomever is necessary but doesn't formally assign anyone else to the job. Although all the department heads promise to help and everyone knows how important the study is, the manager can't get anyone to do the necessary work in time. The project falls further and further behind.

The CEO looks at the results and the manager's performance and concludes that there is a performance (or people) problem. The reality is that since the CEO gave the manager responsibility without authority, **the CEO set the manager up for failure.** Responsibility without authority is a structural and therefore an operational problem. Many otherwise talented managers get sacrificed because their bosses miss this point.

Even though the output variables (or symptoms) of this situation point in the people direction, the causal variables of the situation are clearly operational (the structure is flawed because the manager was given responsibility with no authority). This calls for an entirely different set of alternatives from which to choose a solution.

This chapter looks at the three categories of problems and then introduces a practical, seven-step approach to problem solving and decision making.

People Problems

People problems include all the problems of management that at the causal level are triggered primarily by human behavior. In other words, the source of the problem is usually the action of an individual or a group of people.

People problems can be further categorized into five subcategories:

1. *Intrapersonal.* These are problems within an individual. A good example is a person who loses his personal motivation to do the job. Another example is someone with a skill deficiency

who cannot perform a task she is asked to do because she doesn't know how to do it. Another dimension is added to this classification of problems when we make a distinction between problem employees and troubled employees. *Problem employees* are employees whose performance or behavior on the job causes a problem that needs to be addressed. *Troubled employees* are employees whose performance or behavior on the job causes a problem that needs to be addressed, *but whose problem behavior can be attributed to some ongoing or underlying cause that will probably be best addressed through the use of outside professional help.* Examples of troubled employees include employees who are alcoholics, drug abusers, or addicted to gambling; others may be suffering from depression, serious grief over the loss of a loved one, or other mental or emotional conditions.

2. *Interpersonal.* These are problems between two people. The problem can be something as simple as a breakdown in communications, but it can also be something more complicated, such as a misunderstanding of roles and responsibilities that leads to ongoing conflict. So-called personality clashes are another example of this type of problem.

3. *Intragroup.* These are problems that occur within a group of people. An example is a morale problem that adversely affects an entire work group, department, division, or company. Another example is a project team that consistently fails to meet its deadlines or objectives.

4. *Intergroup.* These are problems that exist between two or more groups. A typical example is when such intense resentment builds up between a line and a staff department that the final results suffer. This type of problem can exist on a relatively small scale, as when two project teams compete with each other in nonsupportive ways, or on a very large scale, as when engineering battles with quality control in ways that put the company at great risk in the marketplace.

5. *Individual vs. Organization.* These are problems that exist between an individual member of the organization and some aspect of the organization's systems and structures or policies. A simple example is when an employee's payroll record keeps getting fouled up because of a processing flaw. A more compli-

cated example is when conflict results from fundamental differences in values between an employee and the company. The employee may feel the company isn't doing enough to protect the environment or isn't meeting its other social obligations.

Most people problems are more tactical than strategic. However, strategic people problems do occur. Institutionalized discrimination, for example, on the basis of race or sex, is an example of a strategic-level people problem that has caused many organizations serious legal problems over the past few decades. Serious labor relations problems, say, with a major trade union, make up another category.

Operational Problems

Operational problems are problems involving the basic systems, processes, and structure of the organization. Usually, they are more tangible than people problems, making it easier for the problem solver to isolate and analyze the variables in the problem. Where the dynamics of human behavior often seem vague and the causes ambiguous, the substance of operational problems is usually more concrete.

Operational problems occur on both the tactical and the strategic level, in about equal numbers. The difference is that the strategic-level problems require considerably more time and are usually more complex.

The following is a fairly common example of a tactical-level operational problem:

> A company recently has purchased a new computer system. Although it is an excellent system and is widely used, it works better for some departments and work groups than it does for the customer service department. There are much better systems that are both simpler and less expensive that would more fully meet customer service's needs.
>
> When the customer service department head raised this issue with upper management, it brushed

the concerns aside, saying that this was the system the company would use. The more customer service uses the system, however, the more it becomes obvious that a great deal of time and money are being wasted in the department because of the system.

This case points to another phenomenon that is especially true of operational problems. That is, most problems are the result of previous solutions! The problems in customer service are a direct result of management's previous decision to implement a new computer system. Although troubleshooting is discussed later in this chapter and again in more detail in Chapter 7, it is important to realize its significance as a step in the problem-solving process from the beginning. If top management in this case had been effective in troubleshooting their initial decision, chances are that the problem in customer service could have been avoided entirely.

To find excellent examples of strategic-level operational problems, pick up a copy of *Business Week, The Wall Street Journal,* or just about any other business-related publication. Many strategic-level operational problems make it into the popular business press because these are the ones that have the greatest impact on business performance and usually make for interesting reading.

Technical Problems

Although many technical problems are extremely difficult and challenging to solve, this category is probably the easiest to understand. The responsible manager's primary emphasis is not on developing new technology or new science in response to technical problems. Rather, it is on the management, or results-producing, aspects of the situation.

Most technical problems are tactical rather than strategic. Here's an example of a tactical-level technical problem.

A medium-size plastics company manufactures a special foam laminate product that is blown thin and attached to carpet padding so that the padding will slide easily during installation. A larger than average number of sample tests were conducted, and all met with extremely positive customer satisfaction. But, two weeks after going into full production, sporadic complaints started coming back from the customers. About a tenth of the laminate was bad. It simply didn't work the way it was supposed to, causing problems during installation. When the sample batches were reevaluated, they were found to be completely problem-free. The other 90 percent of the product remained problem-free. The problem-solving process revealed that the cleaning system used on some of the equipment was bad, causing all the product manufactured after a certain quantity to be faulty.

An example of a strategic-level technical problem is the situation car manufacturers encounter when they discover a safety-related manufacturing defect in a particular model. Depending on when in the production cycle the defect was discovered, the problem could have implications well beyond the manufacturing plant. Class action lawsuits, expensive recalls, individual liability claims, and intervention by regulatory agencies could be part of the equation.

Characteristics of Problems

One way to categorize problems is according to the degree of specificity associated with each. Problems that are vague, ambiguous, somewhat intangible, and with less clear-cut factors associated with them would be at one end of the continuum. Problems with very specific data and data relationships would be at the other.

People problems generally fall at the less specific end of the continuum and technical problems at the opposite end. Operational problems are generally somewhere in the middle. These relationships are shown in the following table:

People	Operational	Technical
Less specific		Very specific
Unclear relationship		factors
Intangible		Tangible
Ambiguous		Unambiguous
Vague		Well-defined

This is an important distinction, because it can predetermine the appropriate mind-set for the problem solver. When working with problems at the less tangible end of the continuum, the problem solver has to possess a high tolerance for ambiguity to be effective. The reverse is true when working at the opposite, more specific end of the continuum.

Engineers, scientists, and people with similar technical backgrounds find it very difficult as a rule to develop a tolerance for ambiguity. Thus, they are inhibited when confronted with operational and people problems to the left on the continuum.

Managers with roots in other areas suffer a reverse dynamic when confronted with technical problems or problems that lie in the more tangible and specific areas of the continuum. They have a tendency to take a surface-level approach, trying a little bit of everything to solve the problem. They will have trouble applying the discipline necessary to stick with an analytical process that will lead to a specific cause and a clear-cut solution.

A sort of mental nimbleness is therefore essential for effective problem solving. The problem solver must know when to tolerate higher levels of ambiguity and still forge ahead and when to be rigid and stubborn, choosing not to proceed until certain details are fully understood.

Tactical vs. Strategic Problems

Tactical problems occur more frequently, take less time to solve, and by themselves are unlikely to threaten the long-term success of the business. Often, they are solved by one person. However, this doesn't mean that they aren't important. They are important because, if they're not dealt with, they could result in lost business, customer dissatisfaction, poor morale, and a lot of money spent unnecessarily.

Strategic problems are broader in scope, affect major segments—if not all—of the organization, and are directly related to the organization's long-term direction and success. Strategic problems are usually more complicated, take more time to solve, and require the input and participation of several people. The solutions to strategic problems usually aren't as easy to derive as tactical solutions, and they require a great deal more judgment.

The Lyles Seven-Step Method

One of the most widely used and most practical approaches to management problem solving and decision making is the Lyles Seven-Step Method. This method has been taught to more than 23,000 managers around the world. The method offers the following benefits:

- It is practical and can be used to solve both tactical and strategic problems.
- It is free from jargon.
- It uses the same basic steps for both decision making and problem solving.
- It is adaptable, lending itself to both simple and complicated problems and decisions.
- It is anticipatory, forcing analysis of future consequences and results.

Figure 5-1 shows the steps in the Lyles Seven-Step Method and how they apply to problem solving and decision making.

Perhaps the greatest overall benefit of the Lyles Method is that it is usable in both decision making and problem solving. When making a decision, the first step is to define the objective(s). When a problem arises, the first step is to define it in the context of previously defined objectives. Once the problem is defined, then the same process is followed to decide what to do about it.

Another important framework for understanding the method is that the first steps (down to and including developing

Figure 5-1. The Lyles seven-step method.

PROBLEM SOLVING	DECISION MAKING
Define the problem.	
Define objective(s).	Define objective(s).
Generate alternatives.	Generate alternatives.
Develop action plan.	Develop action plan.
Troubleshoot.	Troubleshoot.
Communicate.	Communicate.
Implement.	Implement.

an action plan) focus on arriving at the desired "answer," while the last three steps (troubleshoot, communicate, and implement) focus on ensuring that the desired "result" is produced. Figure 5-2 illustrates the two-part nature of the method.

We can now examine each of the seven steps in terms of their individual outcomes.

Step 1: Define the Problem

The first step in the problem-solving process is to ensure that whatever is causing us concern is fully understood and stated in a clear manner so that others can also understand our concern *as it relates to our hierarchy of purpose*. Responsible managers always define problems in a context of accomplishment. When problems arise, they are likely to ask, "How does this affect my results?"

For managers, problems are either obstacles or deviations. An obstacle is an event or phenomenon that is preventing some desired result from occurring. A deviation is when something happens other than what was intended to occur.

Problems also contain two elements: cause and effect. Thus, for a problem definition to be complete, it must also contain two elements: a statement describing the undesired effect or symp-

Figure 5-2. Finding the right answer vs. getting the right results.

Step 1	
plus	Define the problem
Step 2	
plus	Define objective(s)
Step 3	
plus	Generate alternatives
Step 4	
EQUALS the Right Answer	Develop action plan
plus	
Step 5	
plus	Troubleshoot
Step 6	
plus	Communicate
Step 7	
EQUALS the Right Result	Implement

tom, and a statement describing the cause that is creating the undesired effect. If the problem is an obstacle, the undesired effect is that the desired effect is not being achieved.

Thus, a simple, yet complete, format for a problem definition statement would be as follows:

A [*something*]
is causing
B [*some undesirable effect*].

Following this format, a clear definition of a specific problem might read:

Frequent equipment breakdowns in the plant
are causing
late shipments, quality problems with our
products, and low morale.

To check your definition of a problem, be sure that it describes both a cause and an effect. In the above example, the problem is not only late shipments, bad quality, and low morale. Nor is the problem only equipment breakdowns. The problem includes both elements—the equipment failures that are the cause of the problem and the late shipments, bad quality, and low morale that result. Unless both cause and undesired effect are included in the definition, it is incomplete.

Also note that the definition of a problem describes only an undesirable effect and its cause; the definition doesn't imply any solutions to the problem.

The causes of problems are not always readily apparent. More detailed guidelines for identifying causes and sorting out effects are presented in Chapter 6.

Step 2: Define Objective(s)

The first step in decision making and the second step in problem solving is to define objectives—the outcome you would like to achieve as a result of solving the problem or making the decision.

Objectives specify only the outcome you would like to achieve. The action plan, which is developed in Step 4, specifies the means by which you hope to achieve this outcome. An objective might follow this format:

To [*action verb*]
[*single key result*] **by** [*date*]
at [*cost*].

Following this format, a clear definition of objectives for the specific problem with equipment breakdowns might read:

> **To** *reduce the number of equipment breakdowns*
> *in the plant by 90 percent,* **by** *the end of*
> *90 days from now,* **at** *a cost not*
> *to exceed 120 hours of*
> *equipment operator's time and $75,000.*

Of course, the number and format of objectives may vary according to the definition of the problem and your priorities, but this simple format is a good starting point.

Step 3: Generate Alternatives

This is the solution-generating step of the process. In this step, you generate as many alternative ways as you can think of to achieve the objectives you defined in Step 2. For example, a list of alternative ways to solve the breakdown problem might look like this:

Replace all equipment.
Train operators better.
Do preventive maintenance.
Problem solve with operators.
Extend shipping dates.
Review Quality Control
  procedures.
Hire an outside consultant.
Pay operators piece rates.
Change product lines.

Hire all new operators.
Implement a TQM
  program.
Offer better incentives.
Move the plant.
Fire the supervisors.
Evaluate raw materials.
Change processes.
Review capital plan.

Some of these alternatives are not good ones. However, at this point, generating as many alternatives as you can is useful because some that aren't good may lead you to others that are. Remember, in this step you are only generating alternatives—*not* evaluating them or selecting them.

Step 4: Develop Action Plan

This step has two phases. First, evaluate the alternatives you generated in Step 3 to select one or more as your solution. Second, modify the chosen alternative(s) until an action plan is fully developed.

An outline of a very simple action plan that could be used in the solution of the equipment problem might include the following:

1. Discuss the problem with representative groups of operators and supervisors.
2. Implement a preventive maintenance program.
3. Train all operators and supervisors in the new program.
4. Set specific goals for reducing breakdowns during the next 90 days.
5. Reward the operators and the supervisors for achieving goals.

Step 5: Troubleshoot

Most problems are the result of solutions and decisions. The best way to avoid these additional, unintended problems is to troubleshoot your action plan before you implement it. Troubleshooting the action plan is the most cost-effective and efficient problem solving you can perform as a manager.

Review your action plan in terms of the future, and try to anticipate potential problems. Then modify your action plan to solve these problems or bypass them before they occur or become potential crises.

In troubleshooting your action plan for the equipment problem, you might anticipate some of these potential problems:

- The equipment may be too old for preventive maintenance to make a difference.
- The operators may not care enough to provide valid input.
- The rewards you offer may not be meaningful to the operators.

There may be others you can think of. It is then up to you, as the problem solver, to decide which of these potential problems are serious enough to cause you to modify the action plan.

For those that are less serious, you may simply lay out some contingency plans.

Step 6: Communicate

In this step, determine which individuals or groups might affect the success of your action plan. Then determine the best method for giving them the information necessary to ensure the success of your action plan. You can choose from many methods of communicating to these people the information you want them to have: for example, personal visits, telephone calls, memos, letters, audiotapes, fax messages, videotapes, and computer messages.

For different people, you specify different communication objectives. For the problem in our example, you might outline a simple plan such as this:

Communication Target	Objective
Plant manager's boss	Seek advice. Gain support.
Supervisors	Seek advice. Seek leadership. Seek input.
Personnel rep	Seek advice.
Operators	Seek information. Seek feedback.

Step 7: Implement

This final step in problem solving and decision making involves more than merely starting the action. You haven't solved a problem or made a successful decision until you have achieved all the objectives you defined. Therefore, implementation involves follow-up and monitoring through the completion of every objective your action plan specifies.

In the case of the equipment breakdown, starting the action is simple. But follow-up and monitoring results are an important part of implementation.

Six Additional Factors That Affect Results

Imagine a golfer playing a round of golf. If the golfer is typical, he follows a consistently repetitive pattern of behavior. A typical pattern might be: (1) assess the lie of the ball, (2) choose a club, (3) take a practice swing, and (4) hit the ball. This pattern would be repeated with each shot. In fact, it's likely that if any of these steps were skipped, the shot would suffer negative consequences as a result. These steps are necessary for consistent, sustained, effective performance.

However, they're not sufficient. There are other factors that affect the results. Any good golfer will verify that, among other things, it's also important to keep an eye on the ball, keep the leading arm straight, and follow through. These are just as important as the other parts of the pattern are to the success of the shot.

This is an excellent metaphor for problem solving. The seven steps of our problem-solving method are like the four steps of the golf swing. They're necessary, but not necessarily sufficient. There are a number of other factors that the responsible manager must keep in mind when carrying out the seven steps, or else the solution might be missed completely.

Six of these factors stand out as being absolutely critical to the successful implementation of the seven steps. They are like keeping your eye on the golf ball and keeping your leading arm straight. We must keep them foremost in our minds as we work through the problem-solving process. If we miss something with any of these factors, it's likely we'll corrupt the entire problem-solving process. These six factors are:

1. *Gathering the right data*—that is, the information necessary to help understand and optimize each step of the problem-solving and decision-making process
2. *Analyzing the data properly*—interpreting and drawing correct conclusions from the information available
3. *Developing valid insights*—drawing correct conclusions without necessarily having conclusive data
4. *Timing actions properly*—carrying out activities (both

problem-solving activities and solution-related action steps) within appropriate time frames, going neither too fast nor too slow

5. *Thinking critically*—maintaining a constructive, proactive, and questioning approach to each situation
6. *Assessing politics*—accurately evaluating the less tangible, more covert philosophies, biases, and preferences that exist inside the organization, or that may affect it from the outside

These factors must be kept in mind throughout the seven-step process and cannot effectively be addressed by making them a single step in the process. For example, there are some problem-solving and decision-making approaches that list data gathering as a single step in the process. Their approach would be to gather all the facts first, then decide. This is unrealistic because any responsible problem solver gathers data throughout the process. She will be gathering one kind of data when defining the problem ("What's wrong and what caused it?"), a different kind of data when defining objectives ("What opportunities exist and what's possible?"), and still different data during each of the remaining steps. Even during the final step, implementation, the responsible problem solver is still gathering data—trying to determine what is working and what isn't and what problems are arising during implementation.

The same is true of each of the six factors. Different problems are characterized by varying needs to consider each of the factors. Some problems require great sensitivity to political assessment, others none at all. Some require more emphasis on one of the factors at one step rather than another. But all six of the factors can potentially come into play during any of the seven steps. So the effective problem solver must be ready to respond to the needs of each problem relative to each of these factors.

6

Getting the Right Answer

As explained in Chapter 5, one of the major characteristics of the Lyles Seven-Step Method is that the first four steps focus primarily on developing the right answer (or optimal solution) to a problem, while the last three steps focus on achieving the desired result(s) with the identified answer (see Figure 5-2). Although responsible managers are always concerned primarily with producing results, it is imperative that the foundation for achieving those results (an optimal solution) be developed first. This chapter provides detailed guidance for completing each of the first four steps of the Lyles Seven-Step Method.

Step 1: Defining the Problem

What is a problem? The answers we received in response to this question are fascinating. One of the most common is "something that needs an answer." But perhaps the most interesting point is that very few people can precisely define the word *problem* in practical terms, especially as it relates to management. In order to define problems accurately, it is important to know what they are.

Important Premises for Defining the Problem

Problems are one of two things: (1) obstacles, conditions, or phenomena that *stand in the way* of achieving the desired objectives, or (2) obstacles, conditions, or phenomena that *are causing a devi-*

ation from the desired status. The common characteristic of both is that they describe undesirable factors that must be dealt with if the desired organizational results are to be achieved. As discussed in Chapter 5, these factors can be human, operational, or technical in nature. Because of their undesirability, they must be eliminated, circumnavigated, or their adverse effects minimized or neutralized. In order to do any of these things, however, the problems must first be understood.

Defining the problem means to *identify and state* what is causing the desired results not to be achieved or the undesired results to occur. Problems exist when something is wrong. A problem is well defined when the manager sufficiently comprehends what is wrong as to be able to tell others about the situation in terms they can understand *and* to be able to generate possible solutions that will eliminate the problem.

Problems always exist in a context of results. All management activity starts with a decision to accomplish something, to produce certain results. Thus, conditions, events, or phenomena can be classified as problems only when they are either: (1) preventing the attainment of desired objectives, or (2) causing deviations from a desired level of performance.

Another important premise regarding problem definition has to do with the logic of cause and effect. Logic tells us that when something happens, there is a specific cause that made it happen. For example, you go out to your car in the morning and notice that a tire is flat. Something had to have happened to cause the tire to go flat. The same can be said of any occurrence. If it happened, it was because something caused it to happen; there was a cause or a reason for the resulting effect.

Focusing on cause rather than effect can make a big difference in the final results achieved. The most effective solutions are those that deal with the cause rather than the effect. Go back to the flat tire example. Maybe you defined the problem as: "There is no air in the tire." If you apply strict logic based on that definition of the problem, then the obvious solution is "Put air in the tire."

Will the solution work? It all depends. If there is no air in the tire because some kids in the neighborhood let the air out, then the solution will work. However, if the tire is flat because of a nail puncture, then the solution won't work. Identifying the cause enables us to solve the problem correctly.

Desired Outcome of Defining the Problem

Since problems are either obstacles or deviations, one of two simple formats should suffice for the problem statement. Figure 6-1 shows both formats. The first example would be used when an obstacle was preventing the accomplishment of already established goals. The second would be used when something was causing undesired effects to occur.

Specific Approach to Defining the Problem

A simple and straightforward method for defining problems is to follow these three steps:

1. Determine whether the problem is an obstacle or a deviation.
2. State the results portion of the problem definition statement.
3. Identify and state the cause.

Sometimes you'll be able to zip through these three steps in a matter of minutes or even seconds. However, you might spend

Figure 6-1. Problem definition formats.

OBSTACLE

[_____] is preventing [_____].

DEVIATION

[_____] is causing [_____].

hours, days, or even weeks on more complicated problems, which tend to be strategic problems. However, don't abandon the method when tackling more complicated strategic problems. This would make the problem-solving process more muddled (and therefore more challenging), less efficient, and less effective.

Potential Obstacles in Defining the Problem

The most common obstacle encountered while attempting to carry out the first step of the problem-defining technique is that it's often difficult to focus on specific results because there are so many different ones that are of concern. Consider the following example:

> For the past six months a company has been losing sales. Earnings and cash flow are down, and morale is low. On the surface, this problem might look as if it has a simple and straightforward definition related to the sagging sales. However, things are not that simple. A number of different factors are probably contributing to the decline, but there are also more factors to consider. What about the effects of reduced cash flow on production? And what about the morale issue? Is it serious enough to cause matters to get even worse?

The best way to deal with this problem is to *separate* the various components of the problem, to *prioritize* them, and then to deal with them individually where possible. If product quality is a concern, then declining product quality becomes the undesired result in one problem statement. If declining morale is another concern, then that becomes another undesired result in another problem statement. And so on through the list of undesired results (or desired results *not* produced) until all facets of the problem are addressed.

The next most common obstacle to achieving accurate problem definitions is not being able to identify the cause of the problem accurately and specifically. When this occurs, the tendency is to want to charge ahead with the problem-solving process anyway in the hope that whatever solution is developed will deal with the cause in some way.

Responsible managers exercise patience at this point. They continue to work on the problem definition until they've found the cause, knowing that a problem well defined is half the battle. They also know that by focusing on the true cause with their action plans and solutions, they will be more effective and will substantially lower the odds of creating still further problems.

One way to identify an elusive cause is to identify the differences between the problem situation that is not working and similar situations that are working properly. If something is producing one result here and another somewhere else, then there has to be some difference that is causing the different outcome. A simple example is where two machines in a plant are turning out product, but the product from one is flawed. Logic tells you that something in the two machines has to be different for them to produce these different results. To identify the cause, you should analyze the differences between the two machines until you find the difference that explains the results.

Another way to identify elusive causes is to reconstruct a series of events until you have enough evidence to tell you what produced the undesired result. For example, this is the approach used when a commercial airliner crashes.

However, the final test of the definition should always be whether it can fit into the problem definition format. Does it contain both a cause and a results statement? Does the results statement identify your most important concerns? Does the cause statement accurately describe what is creating the result?

Step 2: Defining Objectives

Because the business world changes constantly, the objectives of management ought to be under constant scrutiny to determine if they are still valid in light of the latest circumstances. New information and new circumstances will drive the need for new objectives and new directions. Although this is not always the case, it is true in enough situations to warrant a review and reassessment of those objectives affected by problems and decisions when you confront those problems and decisions.

The objectives of management and the overall goals of the organization should not change with every passing problem or decision. However, it is critically important that each manager know exactly how the solution to every problem and the result of each decision relate to the organization's hierarchy of objectives.

Important Premises for Defining Objectives

When solving problems and making decisions, objectives should be defined on two levels. First, the manager should define the overall objective, the key results to be achieved in this area of management responsibility. Second, the manager should decide what the objectives of this particular management action are. A large number of needless problems could be avoided if managers would take at least a short time to review their objectives in the light of current circumstances rather than rush to the solution without using objectives to guide them. This is the one shortcut that in the long run always turns out to be a long cut.

Once the problem has been defined and the current predicament and its cause are fully understood, you can concentrate on setting objectives. A number of options exist, the most obvious of which include:

1. Trying to go from where you are now to the desired results that were initially defined
2. Restoring circumstances to the point at which they departed from the original path, then proceeding toward the initial desired results
3. Changing the overall objectives and proceeding to try to accomplish a completely new set of desired results
4. Abandoning this set of desired results completely and dedicating your resources elsewhere

Guidelines for Defining Objectives

Until the application of these guidelines becomes second nature, it is a good idea to review them before beginning any problem-solving or decision-making activity.

1. *If there is a problem involved, make sure you understand it completely before attempting to formulate objectives.* Don't try to decide where you want to go until you understand pretty well where you are.

2. *Avoid discussing answers, solutions, and methods until objectives are clearly defined.* Objectives should address results and intended outcomes and should stay away from the "how to."

3. *Proactively reassess objectives and seek new ones.* Assume that you don't know everything, that you are surrounded by new opportunities just waiting to be discovered, and that your current opinions are probably obsolete.

4. *Question everything by not taking anything for granted.* Frequently the most exciting opportunities are uncovered by asking "naive" questions about the most mundane subjects or events.

5. *Don't waste time setting objectives for things that are going to happen anyway.* The value of objectives is that they serve as tools to cause things to happen that would not otherwise occur.

6. *Be specific.* Focus as much as possible on measurable factors, tangible end results, and quantifiable outcomes. Also be as specific as possible regarding times and deadlines. Don't say you want "to do something better as soon as possible." Instead, say you want "to improve productivity an average of 10 percent per worker on all three production lines within six months."

7. *Make sure that the objectives you set are always feasible.* They should challenge people but not be beyond the limits of what can realistically be accomplished. Setting objectives that are not feasible destroys your credibility.

Be reasonably consistent. (This does not mean that you should be rigid and inflexible.) Consistency should appear on several levels. New objectives should be consistent with previous objectives, with those of higher management as well as with those of your peers and subordinates, and with your own managerial responsibilities. Your objectives should also be consistent with existing organizational policy and practices and with the available resources, including money, manpower, machine time, available time, facilities, and talent.

Desired Outcome for Defining Objectives

The most commonly accepted format for objectives is that developed by management theorist George Morrisey some two decades ago.[1] Objectives should follow this format, which contains four major elements: To [*action or accomplishment verb*] [*single key result*] by [*target date*] at [*cost*]. Here are some examples:

> To regain 100 percent of our lost market share in the Colorado consumer photofinishing market by the end of this fiscal year at a cost not to exceed $100,000 and 240 hours of marketing and sales staff time.

> To reduce our packaging costs by 10 percent by July 31 at a cost not to exceed 60 work hours.

> To implement a plantwide preventive maintenance program for all manufacturing equipment by October 15 at a cost not to exceed 160 work hours.

If, in the rare circumstances that you need more information to help clarify your intentions, stick with this format and add an amplifying paragraph underneath rather than amend the format of the objective itself.

Potential Obstacles in Defining Objectives

The greatest potential obstacle in defining objectives is sloppiness in their derivation. Unclear objectives—objectives that fail to focus energy and attention on specific results—are of no value. To overcome this obstacle, Morrisey again offers the best advice. The following are modified versions of his suggested questions for evaluating objectives:

- Is the objective constructed properly?
- Is it measurable and verifiable?
- Does it relate to the responsible manager's role and mission and to higher-level roles, missions, and objectives?
- Is it readily understood?
- Is it realistic and attainable?

- Will the result justify the cost?
- Is it consistent with basic policy and practice?
- Is accountability for results clearly established?[2]

Step 3: Generating Alternatives

Generating alternatives involves much more than merely thinking up things to do. There is a difference between activities that seem like reasonably worthwhile endeavors and alternative courses of action that are devised specifically to contribute to the accomplishment of managerial objectives.

Important Premises for Generating Alternatives

Two factors make the difference in generating meaningful alternatives. The first is the presence of goal orientation and the focus on results. Alternatives gain their value when it is clear that they will lead to the accomplishment of important end results.

The second factor has to do with creativity. Most problems and nonproblem situations in management are unique. There is always something in a particular set of circumstances that differs from the characteristics of previous similar circumstances. Thus, being able to create on an ongoing basis is the key to generating viable alternatives.

Specific Approaches to Generating Alternatives

The most common technique used to generate alternatives is brainstorming. Although usually a group process, the same techniques can be used by individuals acting alone. The key to success, whether acting alone or with a group, is discipline— rigorously following the ground rules.

Brainstorming

Brainstorming is used to generate creative ideas as to possible alternative courses of action that serve as raw material or "input" in the development of an action plan. It works best with groups of less than ten. The process is very simple. The group starts by making sure that every member fully understands the objectives of the decision and has a common vision regarding the desired end results. The members then begin thinking up alternative ways to accomplish the objectives. As the alternatives are generated, one or two members of the group write them down (on a chalkboard or flip-chart for all to see) as quickly as possible and just *as stated* by the originator. This part of the process should be intense and uninhibited, with everyone trying to develop as many new and different ideas as possible. It is best to avoid discussion or evaluation of individual ideas as they are presented because this will slow down the process and dampen enthusiasm and creativity. Here are five ground rules for brainstorming sessions. Post them in the meeting room, review them at the start of the session, and refer to them whenever any of them is being violated during the session.

1. Do your best to develop as many new and different alternatives as possible.
2. Adopt an "anything goes" approach. There is no such thing as a "bad" idea. A far-out and impractical suggestion may spur a creative and practical idea by someone else.
3. Don't evaluate, criticize, or discuss any of the ideas during the brainstorming process.
4. Use the ideas of others to stimulate your own thinking. Try to improve on them or combine them so as to come up with better approaches.
5. Encourage each other. Work as a group to develop a group product rather than competing with each other.

There are a number of techniques that can be used during the brainstorming process to stimulate creative thinking. Rather than presenting these to the group all at once, the group leader should mention a couple at a time when there are lulls in the idea-generating activities. These techniques for thinking along different dimensions can be triggered by asking the following questions:

• *Can we combine?* Which of the ideas or alternatives can be blended together or combined? Can an assortment of alternatives be devised so that the total effect will be different from the individual parts?

• *What existing things can be modified to meet this need?* Can we change the shape, name, sound, odor, taste, movement, sequence, or color of the product?

• *Can we magnify anything to create different alternatives?* Can something be added? What about enlargements, additional ingredients, or greater frequency?

• *What can be reduced?* Is it possible to subtract or eliminate something to develop additional options? Can something be made smaller or lighter? Slower or less frequent? Can something be split up or divided into smaller units, steps, or parts?

• *Are any opposites feasible?* What happens when we reverse direction on something? How about working backward? Can we turn something inside out or upside down?

• *Can we think of any substitutes?* What if someone else did it? What other equipment is practical? How about different times or places?

Sequential solicitation is yet another technique to enhance brainstorming. It is designed to provide each member of the group with an opportunity to contribute; it also tends to force presentation of ideas that members might otherwise be reluctant to propose. The recorders merely solicit ideas from each member in sequence by going around the room, giving each member an opportunity to speak in order. If a member has nothing to suggest on a given turn, she just says "pass" and works on developing an idea for the next turn. Although this procedure makes the process less spontaneous, it also makes it difficult for a small number of group members to dominate the discussion. It forces discussion to focus more directly on the problem, promotes greater involvement, and discourages members from developing one "good" idea and then dropping out.

After the group runs dry—that is, no more new ideas are forthcoming—there are still several things that can be done to further stimulate thinking. One method, often referred to as the second effort technique, works as follows. Have the entire group sit or mill about the room in absolute silence, reviewing and studying all the alternatives that have been suggested so far. At the end of three minutes, require everyone to take one more minute to develop one more idea. Then go around the room soliciting this one additional idea from each person. Quite often the very best ideas are generated during this reflective period.

Individual and Group Accumulation

A second method of generating alternatives is called individual and group accumulation. It is somewhat similar to brainstorming, but the differences are substantial.

Individual and group accumulation calls for having each person individually "accumulate" as many ideas/alternatives as possible before sharing anything with the group. This individual accumulation is usually accomplished by simply having everyone quietly and individually list all the alternatives they can think of on a sheet of paper. After everyone has done this, the group then "accumulates" all the individual ideas by each person sharing his or her ideas, one at a time, until all the ideas are gathered. During the group accumulation phase, only questions of clarification are allowed. The group then discusses the ideas, builds on them, and adds more to the list.

The major difference between accumulation and brainstorming is that accumulation forces everyone to participate and gives all participants a more equal standing in the process. This is not always achieved in brainstorming, where the quickest thinkers and most verbal people tend to dominate the process.

A second major advantage is that the group is less likely to go down a specific path together. Often during brainstorming, one or two people offer their first suggestions, and those suggestions create a framework or perspective in everyone else's mind that limits the scope of the ideas generated. If everyone works independently first, the group is much more likely to consider a larger number of perspectives and not be bound by a limited number of mental frameworks.

Potential Obstacles in Generating Alternatives

The most common problem in generating alternatives is for people to become bogged down by their previous experiences. This causes the brainstorming session to be more of a memory-testing exercise than an exercise in creativity. Recalling old techniques is not necessarily bad, but if it is the only source of ideas, the results are bound to be bland and boring. Brainstorming is most effective when it fosters creativity and the development of *new and different* courses of action.

One of the most important rules to remember when generating alternatives is one that is used specifically for brainstorming. The rule is that evaluation and criticism should be avoided until after all alternatives have been developed. Only then should the actual deciding take place.

Step 4: Developing Action Plans

This is the step in the process in which the most important deciding takes place.

Important Premises for Developing Action Plans

Regardless of the strategy or type of problem or decision under scrutiny, there are ten commandments that should be followed:

1. *Focus on the total end result to be achieved.* One manufacturing manager expressed his frustration with his company's decision-making practices as follows: "The problem around here is that people decide to start doing things before they ever get a clear picture of where we're going. The result is we're constantly changing direction and making modifications to the extent that our company's manufacturing philosophy could best be described as 'pound to fit and paint to match.' If only once we could know for sure where we were headed before we started, we'd be a heck of a lot more productive."[3]

2. *Never accept your final choice as being final.* New information, events, and circumstances drive new decisions. Many managers feel that reversing or changing a decision after it has been announced will be interpreted as a demonstration of poor planning or indecisiveness. But frequently a course of action that was sound when first decided on becomes unsound owing to changing circumstances. The consequences of steadfastly following an unsound course of action could be worse than any repercussions from changing it.

3. *Choose an alternative other than the first one thought of at least 80 percent of the time.* First solutions are almost never the best ones. For this reason, it is best to defer acceptance of the first solution until as many alternatives as possible have been thought of and examined.

4. *Choose actions that are clearly justified by the demands of the current situation.* Don't do anything solely because it worked once before. Problems that appear to be similar on the surface most often prove to be radically different when analyzed in depth. In any but the most static organizations, priorities and directions change with time, making the demands of apparently similar problems quite different.

5. *Never follow the advice of experts unless the advice makes complete sense to you.* Experts in a particular field typically became expert because they studied a specialty. As such, they tend to take a limited view of problems. Managers today must frequently solicit expert advice in certain areas. However, this advice should not automatically decide the course of action. The manager should ultimately decide the course of action on the basis of what makes sense to her personally, after having tempered the expert advice with her own experience and current knowledge of the organization's needs and priorities.

6. *Always pay attention to your own intuitions or hunches.* A hunch is a conclusion based on facts you have previously observed and stored. If you've accumulated facts and information about this type of situation in the past, and if you have found out all you can about the current situation, and as a result you have a strong hunch, you should probably go with it. Intuition and hunches are different from hopes and wishful thinking.

7. *Always be prepared to deal with new circumstances and information.* Remember that once you act, things will change. It is virtually impossible in large, complex organizations to act without triggering some kind of reaction that will alter the situation in some meaningful way. Take this dynamic into account when developing action plans.

8. *Be bold rather than timid in the knowledge that major changes are easier to implement and more likely to take hold than minor changes.* Norms are to organizations what habits are to individuals. Once these comfortable patterns of behavior are established, it is difficult to nudge people away from them. But if you disrupt the entire routine of the organization, then carefully manage the settling-in process, you are much more likely to achieve lasting and meaningful change.

9. *Assess the needs and priorities of those around you and design your action plan to be supportive of them.* Tie your goals, objectives, and action plans into those of your associates. Attempt to create synergy by building other people's goals into your action plan.

10. *Take plenty of time to decide.* Haste does tend to make waste (particularly in management decisions), so don't rush things. Of course, many decisions can be made immediately, and making some decisions late is the same as not making them at all. On the other hand, important decisions should not be rushed. Some situations improve with time, and frequently our understanding of certain situations and of the alternatives to them improves with time as well.

Although these factors do not guarantee success in every case, if you are sensitive to these issues, you will definitely improve the overall quality of the action plans you develop.

Specific Approaches to Developing Action Plans

Again, a three-step technique is most valuable. First, narrow the number of your alternatives. Second, select those that optimally satisfy your objectives. Third, develop your action plan using the objectives you've selected.

To reduce a large number of alternatives to a smaller number, first establish several key criteria to evaluate them against. Do this by examining the objectives you set in Step 2 of the overall seven-step method. For example, if timing is important in one or more of your objectives, then one of your criteria should measure how well this timing need is met.

Next, create a table with the alternatives listed down the left side and the criteria listed across the top. Evaluate how well each alternative satisfies each criterion. In a short time you'll be able to identify which alternatives are the strongest and which are the weakest. Select the alternative or subset of alternatives that best satisfies your criteria to form the basis of your action plan.

If you have a smaller number of alternatives, you may wish to use a force-field analysis to weigh the advantages and disadvantages of each. Write each alternative across the top of a piece of paper, then divide the remainder of the paper into two columns, labeled pro and con. (If working with a group, do this on a flip-chart.) On each sheet, list all arguments in favor of choosing an alternative in the pro column and the arguments against it in the con column. The alternative with the strongest (not necessarily the most) factors in its favor and the weakest to its detriment should be chosen to form the basis of the action plan.

Potential Obstacles in Developing Action Plans

The most common problem with action plans is that problem solvers often choose a course of action that is not the best. Sometimes this happens because those involved in the decision focus on developing a solution that will satisfy the individual wants and needs (oftentimes ego and ownership needs) of those involved in the decision rather than on developing a solution that will best satisfy the needs and objectives of the problem.

The seven ground rules that follow will help in group decision-making processes:

1. *Actively consider all alternatives.* There is a tendency among groups to gradually drop from discussion, and therefore from active consideration, some of the alternatives originally offered. This can happen without the group's formally deciding to do so, and often without its even being aware that it is happen-

ing. When an alternative is deleted, make sure that this results from a conscious decision.

2. *Actively take into account all criteria and everyone's perspective.* Care must be taken to avoid allowing the personal agendas of one or two group members to dominate the decision-making process.

3. *View differences of opinion as helpful.* When different opinions are presented, there is an enhanced opportunity for learning. Debates cause new information to be presented and almost always lead to a deeper level of understanding by everyone in the group.

4. *Avoid arguing just for the sake of winning the argument.* There is a difference between arguing to get to the truth of the matter (to find out what the best answer really is) and arguing to win your point at any cost (with the foregone conclusion that, no matter what anyone else says, you'll stick by your original opinion). Part of the difference is common sense; another part is being open to influence and being a good listener. But the biggest difference is in the quality of the final results that are achieved. For the best results in the long run, argue as a means of finding the best answer, regardless of whether that answer agrees with your original position.

5. *Don't agree just to be agreeable.* No one in a decision-making group should ever go along with the group when he firmly disagrees with it solely to avoid creating dissonance, tension, or irritation. To do so is single-handedly to abrogate the responsibilities that the individual has to the group. When there are differences of opinion, they should be raised and openly discussed.

6. *Don't take numerical shortcuts.* This entire process can be tedious, time-consuming, and often stressful. Because of this, group members tend to want to take shortcuts, like voting, assigning numerical values, or averaging. If it truly appears that another strategy might be more productive, then use it. If, however, the evaluation process set forth here is the best strategy, then stick with it.

7. *Encourage everyone to participate.* The surest way to subvert the group process is to allow it to proceed without the full

participation of everyone involved. Although it must be recognized that different people participate differently, everyone should have the opportunity to take part in the process in such a way that her unique contribution is taken advantage of. Note, though, that any time group decision-making techniques are employed, the situation should be analyzed first to determine if it will be cost-effective to use a group. If a group is used for no other reason than because everyone wants to take part, then it would be better not to use a group at all.

*   *   *   *   *

Once you've developed an action plan, you're only halfway home. No one will benefit, and the organization will not have progressed, until the action plan is fully implemented, the problem solved, and your objectives achieved. You must successfully complete the last three steps of the method, described in detail in Chapter 7.

Notes

1. George Morrisey, *Management by Objectives and Results* (Reading, Mass.: Addison Wesley, 1970), pp. 87–98.
2. Ibid., pp. 100–101.
3. Statement supplied by Richard Lyles made by participant in a management seminar during 1986 in southern California.

7

Getting the Right Result

Over half the failures that occur in problem solving happen because: (1) there were foreseeable problems that the problem solvers failed to anticipate; (2) communication regarding the proposed course of action was mishandled; or (3) the implementation was botched. Those failures that occur because of bad solutions or poorly developed action plans are clearly in the minority.

Thus, problem solvers need to follow through. It is not enough to produce the right answer, using the first four of the seven steps. You must complete all seven of the steps to produce the right result.

Step 5: Troubleshooting

Troubleshooting should be introduced into a manager's practices in two places. First, it should always be the fifth formal step in problem solving and the fourth formal step in decision making, as outlined in the Lyles Method. Immediately after the action plan is developed, time should be taken for a detailed critical review of the plan to identify potential problems.

Second, troubleshooting should be applied in the ongoing thought processes of the manager's everyday activities. A constant look forward to anticipate potential problems is a wise investment of time and mental energy. In fact, the most efficient problem solving possible is problem solving in advance—taking care of problems before they arise or interfere with anything.

Important Premises for Troubleshooting

Troubleshooting is separate and distinct from the analysis of advantages and disadvantages or the weighing of pros and cons you do when developing an action plan. In that phase of activity, the emphasis was on comparing alternatives to each other, to your objectives, or to some other criteria.

Now it is time to broaden your perspective and see what potential problems that have not yet been considered are likely to be encountered when your action plan is implemented. Here, you evaluate your action plan in light of the total situation.

Years ago at dances, it was common to hang a ball from the ceiling and rotate it. The ball was about a meter in diameter and covered with little pieces of mirror. As it rotated, light would strike all the different mirrors and reflect dozens of different rays in different directions, creating an ever-changing effect throughout the room. The interaction this multifaceted globe had with its environment comes close to describing the relationship a manager has with the managerial environment. There are dozens of interaction interfaces, each having its own orientation and direction of focus, like the mirrors on the globe. Every time the manager makes a move (shines a light), an effect occurs along every dimension. Some of these effects are good, some are bad, and some don't matter in the overall scheme of things. However, none should be discounted or ignored until the determination has been made that they need not be worried about.

This is where troubleshooting enters the picture. The purpose of troubleshooting is to expand the focus of thinking from the specific parameters within which the decision, problem, or course of action has been considered thus far to include all the possible areas that could be affected when the selected action is taken. It is important that this expanded thinking take potential opportunities into consideration as well as potential problems.

No one can predict for certain any future occurrence. However, based on our understanding of the past and the present, it is possible to formulate some fairly detailed and reasonably reliable predictions about things that are likely to occur. And, of course, by doing certain things today, it is possible for us to increase or decrease the likelihood of certain events in the future.

Responsible managers should do more than make plans and hope that they come true. Instead, they should make plans and do everything possible to make them come true. They must be aggressive in identifying, analyzing, and dealing with every possible factor that could have an effect on the results they intend to achieve.

Specific Approaches to Troubleshooting

Different troubleshooting approaches work better or worse depending on the complexity and comprehensiveness of the action plan. It is often beneficial to have troubleshooting activities carried out by people other than those who developed the action plan. This provides a fresh look from a different perspective that frequently identifies more problems and opportunities. The five most common troubleshooting approaches are: (1) performing a critical review, (2) predicting, (3) testing, (4) exemplifying, and (5) exaggerating.

Critical Review

You perform a critical review when you review the plan by answering the following series of questions:

1. Are the objectives of the plan sound, desirable, and understood?
2. What is the likelihood that the proposed course of action will achieve the objectives?
3. Are staffing plans adequate to carry out the action?
4. Have plans been made to capitalize on collateral advantages? What other benefits might result from the implementation of this plan?
5. Is the plan to communicate detailed enough so that support will be generated and all those affected will know what to expect?
6. What are the disadvantages of the proposed action?
7. In what ways can the course of action fail?
8. Who might want to see it fail?
9. Is the proposed course of action likely to embarrass

anyone such as top management, another department, or customers?

10. Why do anything at all? Why do this?
11. Is the time frame realistic and feasible?
12. Is there a better time to act?
13. Are there special conditions that may have been over-looked that could throw the project off schedule?
14. Why do it this way? Is there a better way?
15. Who else should give approval or be informed of the decision?
16. Is the course of action truly cost-effective? If you were spending your own money, is this how you would spend it?
17. Does anything about the proposed course of action make you feel at all uneasy or uncomfortable?

Routinely answering these questions for all the plans that you are asked to review and approve would eliminate somewhere between 25 percent and 40 percent of the problems that would be encountered if this step were omitted.

Predicting

To predict simply means to estimate as best as possible the most likely consequences of the actions being planned, then to adjust the plan accordingly to reduce the possibility of adverse outcomes and increase the probability of positive results.

Figure 7-1 is a format that can be used to list, evaluate, and analyze different events and actions. The first column is for listing potential problems and opportunities. The second column is for giving some indication of the likelihood that any of these will occur. The third column is for indicating the level of importance or value of each given item. The fourth column is for listing proactive actions that can be taken to increase the probability of any positive impact occurring. The final column is for listing contingency plans that can be set in motion or reactive actions that can be taken in case the problem or opportunity does occur.

Figure 7-1. Format for troubleshooting.

Potential Problems & Opportunities	Probability	Impact	Proactive Action	Reactive Action

Testing

Testing means to actually test the proposed course of action through the use of models, controlled conditions, or a representative sample, under conditions that are not too costly or time-consuming. Test results can then be extrapolated to the total area that will be influenced by the intended actions. In this way, fairly reliable determinations can be made regarding feasibility and potential problems.

You must take great care ascertaining that the data are used with integrity. In other words, tests should be used in decision making or troubleshooting only if they test the actual variables that are being considered. Only those factors that have been tested should be considered as reliable for use in the actual implementation of the plan. Here's an example illustrating how tests can backfire if this rule is violated.

> A fast-food chain specializing in hamburgers decides to test the expansion of its product line by introducing a steak sandwich in some of its restaurants. During the test, a small packet of steak sauce bearing an established brand name and of proven popularity is included with each sandwich. The tests show the steak sandwich to be extremely popular, significantly boosting the sales volume in each restaurant serving it. The test results are reported to top management, which decides to implement the sales of steak sandwiches nationwide. In reviewing the proposal, the chief operating officer notices the relatively high cost of the steak sauce that is included with each sandwich. A similar sauce could be included at a much lower cost. The decision is made to introduce the steak sandwich nationwide using the cheaper sauce. The results are disastrous. Overall sales volume increases during the first month, then drops dramatically. The problem is the steak sauce. People just don't like it, and their level of dislike is sufficient to scare them away from the new sandwich. However, it is too late to do much about it, and the company takes three years recovering from the fiasco.

When using tests, limit the number of factors being tested. Don't test one thing and implement another. If a number of things justify testing, then test them one at a time. Most important, don't overlook the small details.

Exemplifying

To exemplify means to evaluate specific examples of situations that are likely to be encountered when carrying out the intended course of action, to identify potential problems and opportunities before the course of action is implemented.

Consider the situation in which a new policy is being considered for implementation throughout the company. It might be impractical to test the policy as a strategy for troubleshooting. However, it would make a great deal of sense to think of different situations throughout the company where the policy might affect operations, and then think through and analyze exactly what these effects might be. For instance, you might ask how the new policy would affect people in purchasing, finance, or personnel.

Exaggerating

The final method used frequently is that of exaggerating. Quite often, the potential impact of certain issues and events can be better understood if they are blown way out of proportion for the purposes of troubleshooting. Deliberately overstating the events and/or consequences that are likely to occur forces new perspectives or deeper levels of thinking regarding the anticipated outcomes.

Worst-case analysis is one type of exaggeration. It is conducted by simply asking, "What's the worst possible thing that could happen if I do this?" More often than not, when this question is answered in detail, the answer leads to a new perspective regarding the issue at hand. This analysis can also aid substantially in generating alternatives and contingency plans for implementation in the event that things do not turn out the way they were intended.

Exaggerating on the positive side has benefits too. Also ask, "What will we do if things turn out to be substantially better than we predict?" Be prepared to take advantage of unexpected good luck when it occurs.

Step 6: Communicating

Overall effectiveness in problem solving and decision making is a function of both quality and acceptance. It is possible to have an absolutely top-quality solution and still be ineffective if there is no acceptance. No matter how good the solution is, if it is not accepted by those who must support it and act to achieve the final result, the end product will be failure. Communicating focuses on the issues related to gaining acceptance for solutions in order to achieve the optimum final results.

Many excellent solutions and decisions have failed in the past because they were improperly communicated. Consistent achievers have long recognized that having a good idea, a correct solution to a problem, or a valid decision is only half the battle. All is meaningless unless it is acted upon responsibly by others.

Important Premises for Communicating

Good communication and the transfer of understanding don't just happen. Responsible communication in the corporate environment is the result of careful and deliberate planning.

In planning an effective communications strategy, the manager must not assume that others know anything at all about the decision or plan to act. In fact, to be safe, the manager should always assume that others understand even less than they appear to understand. And even understanding is not enough to ensure the desired results.

When communicating an idea:

- Do your homework. Marshal your facts and arguments so that you can communicate the idea in a detailed and hard-hitting presentation.
- Present the idea formally, no matter whom you are presenting to and how informal your relationship with that person might be.
- Make sure there are some benefits to the recipient of your proposal that are likely to cause him to respond favorably *and* help carry out the intended course of action.
- Don't violate the lines of authority, but make sure your plan to communicate will carry your proposal to *all* those who will have a say in approving your idea.

There is no such thing as effective one-way communication. For communication to be effective, information must travel in both directions between sender and receiver. There must be feedback that the initial message was received and understood in the context that was intended. Thus, any plan for communicating must contain a mechanism for feedback and testing so that the person who sent the message knows exactly what effect the message had.

Specific Approaches to Communicating

Figure 7-2 contains a format to use in planning your communications regarding the action plans you develop.

Once your efforts at communicating have paved the way for your plan of action, it is time to act. All that has been discussed up until now is meaningless if the final results are not achieved.

Step 7: Implementing

If organizational performance is to be sustained, then individual managers must be assigned (or must voluntarily acquire) spe-

Figure 7-2. Format for communicating an action plan.

Communication Target (Either a person or a population)	Objective	Mode	By When

cific responsibilities that are theirs alone, not shared with any-one else. Then, their performance must be assessed on the basis of whether they achieve the results incumbent on these responsi-bilities. The first level of assessment is *whether or not* the intended results were achieved. The second level, which is like the frost-ing on the cake, is *how well* the results were achieved. Unfortu-nately, many managers examine accomplishment in just the reverse order. They start with the "how well" evaluation and count any activity aimed at achieving the results as evidence of performance. This may be helpful at times but can also be misleading.

The results that matter most are the final results—the ac-complishment of the intended objectives. That is why implemen-tation is so important. Nothing is worse than seeing an absolutely brilliant solution to a problem fail because the origi-nator figured the battle was over as soon as the idea had been communicated.

One truly fatal assumption a manager can make is that everyone else cares about the idea, recognizes its merit, and is concerned about its accomplishment. Often they don't, and good managers recognize this. Rather than complain or blame others for lack of support, responsible managers do whatever is necessary, short of undermining others, to achieve the results.

Important Premises for Implementing

Implementation means causing changes to occur somewhere in your sphere of influence as a manager. It is impossible to imple-ment any course of action and not have something change as a result. This means that certain things must be disrupted, discon-tinued, or deferred, and new activities must begin. But most im-portant, it means that after you have initiated action, things will be different. The key is in creating exactly the right amount of disruption. The following guidelines should help you to accom-plish the implementation of your action plan with the minimum amount of adverse disruption and the maximum amount of suc-cess.

• *Always implement changes from the top down.* Changes in organizations do not flow up. A common mistake among upper-level managers is to assume that results will be realized if action is first taken at the bottom levels of supervision or among the workforce. This rarely turns out to be the case. The most effective changes take place when an environment has been established that will nurture and support the desired behaviors and activities, and this can be accomplished only if the people in policy-making and key operating positions are on board first.

• *Always start with the best first.* Build on strengths, not weaknesses. If given a choice between implementing a new idea in a really good work group or in one that is struggling along, do it first with the good group. Several reasons justify this. First, it is important that your early results be as positive as possible. Failure off the starting line could doom the entire plan to defeat. Second, you should always attempt to position your best people on the leading edge. The people in your organization should be conditioned to follow winners. Third, these people have earned the opportunity to be innovative. There aren't many better ways to reward good people than by letting them be the pioneers.

• *Set your own example.* Nothing is more convincing than seeing managers doing exactly what they are asking others to do. Nothing will establish new norms more quickly than for the leaders in the organization to start behaving in the desired manner themselves. As part of a strategy for implementation, a manager will often change her own behavior before asking others to do the same, which lends a certain credibility to the request.

• *Remember that you can't motivate people to do something they don't know how to do.* Lack of base-level knowledge and ability are often overlooked factors that doom many good plans to failure. Ensure that your implementation process involves opportunities to acquire any specialized knowledge or skills that do not already exist but that are required for the success of your plan. Consider public seminars, in-house seminars, in-house presentations, informal discussion groups, audio- or videotapes, and self-teaching materials. Whatever the mode, the important factor is making sure that people have the basic ability to do what you ask them to do.

• *Recognize and reward desired performance early.* The overall level of performance, and the level at which the performance is sustained, can be dramatically affected if people are recognized for doing the right things and are rewarded in a manner that is meaningful to them. Any time people do something new, everyone is looking for some signal from the organization or from management that will indicate the extent to which the new behaviors are valued. Send clear and forceful messages as early as possible.

• *Pace implementation so that the timing is consistent with the needs of your plan.* If it takes too long to accomplish your aims, people will lose interest and not take you or your plan seriously. On the other hand, if you push too hard, you may build up a wall of resistance. Each plan is different and requires different timing. Be sensitive to everything else that is happening and to the reactions of those involved. Make sure that things happen at a brisk pace, quickly enough to keep up interest and enthusiasm, but not so quickly as to build up resistance.

• *Provide coaching and follow-up consulting, and, above all, be persistent.* Just because everyone is informed of their responsibilities and your expectations regarding their performance, don't expect that everything you desire will automatically occur. Often, the slightest problem or obstacle will cause others to abandon their efforts on your action plan. In these cases, bring your expertise to bear on solving these minor problems and overcoming the obstacles to successful implementation. You will have to be the persistent one when energy wanes.

Specific Approaches to Implementing

As a general rule, responsible managers delegate some of the implementation tasks to others. However, sometimes circumstances justify doing it yourself. One reason might be that it is necessary to convey to others that you think the action you are taking is important. Another reason might be that it is important for the desired action to be carried out exactly as you want it to be. Rather than run the risk of having someone else deviate from the intended action, it might be better to ensure precision by doing it yourself. A final reason might be urgent time constraints. If immediate action is imperative, doing it yourself is often the most expeditious route.

There are, however, many problems with doing it all yourself:

- You may become overburdened with the details of implementing and thereby deny yourself the opportunity to be a proactive and innovative manager.
- You are withholding responsibilities and meaningful work opportunities from your subordinates.
- You are missing the creative input of those to whom you might delegate certain responsibilities.
- You minimize the opportunities for personal growth, development, and learning on the part of your subordinates.
- You thwart any feelings of team spirit and cohesiveness that might otherwise arise.

As a general rule, which is particularly true the higher up you ascend in the organization, it is better to delegate. This means directing others to accomplish the necessary tasks without your involvement. However, effective delegation is more than merely giving other people work to do. Effective delegation means making meaningful assignments to subordinates that will be both challenging and rewarding. The nine guidelines that follow should be helpful in delegating.

1. *Make sure everyone understands exactly what has been delegated.* All involved should know what they are being held accountable for and what the extent of their individual accountability is.

2. *Make sure only one person is held accountable for each specific result.* Joint or dual accountability is no accountability.

3. *Delegate authority along with accountability and responsibility.* Nothing is more frustrating than to be asked to do something and to be held accountable for accomplishing it but to be denied the tools necessary for its accomplishment. Make sure authority is given when necessary.

4. *Devise an agreed-upon reporting system so that you will know how things are progressing.* Make sure this reporting system has some mechanism for giving early warning of potential problems

so that you can take whatever action is necessary to stave off disaster before it strikes.

5. *Assign milestones and target dates for the accomplishment of specific results.* This way everyone can assume the same degree of urgency regarding the matters under consideration.

6. *Give as much freedom as possible to the people you delegate to.* When possible, focus on results rather than methods.

7. *Make assignments in a motivating and challenging way so as to stimulate as much enthusiasm and excitement as possible.*

8. *Make individual assignments fit the person to the extent that this is possible.* Take into account knowledge, experience, career development needs, training needs, ability, and aptitude.

9. *Always elicit feedback to ensure that everyone involved understands exactly what is expected.*

Potential Obstacles to Implementing

The single most important point to remember is that no matter how good the system is or how sound the method, there is no system or technique that guarantees success. Methods and strategies are useful, but they are only tools and should be recognized as such.

Don't place blind faith in any technique or principle. As soon as you find something that you think will work in all situations, a new set of circumstances will arise that is likely to knock you flat on your back because you will be caught unprepared, having placed too much confidence in your technique.

As long as we have organizations, there will be a need for managers and the functions of management. There is no substitute for the human judgment that is required to make organizations work. And methods, techniques, and even machines don't produce organization results—responsible managers do!

8

Judgment: The Foundation of Responsibility

Judgment is different from decision making. Decision making involves choosing a particular course of action, whereas judgment—the raw material of decision making—is simply drawing an inference from data. Good intentions based on bad judgment still produce bad decisions.

Decisions are not events that take place at a single moment in time. Rather, they are a collection of a series of judgments that have taken place over time. Every decision is the end result of multiple instances of judgment.

When solving problems and making decisions, managers exercise judgment continually on three different levels. First is on the process level, where constant consideration is given to such questions as: "When should I address this problem?" "Who are the best people to get involved?" "Where should I go to find the necessary information?" "How much time should I take gathering data?" There's no pat answer to any of these questions and no formula that will lead you to a perfect approach in every case.

The second level involves making determinations about what is relevant and what is not. Being able to establish parameters, or boundaries around different situations, in order to sustain relevancy is a critical skill.

The third level involves drawing meaning or inferences from data. To reduce complex mental tasks to simple judgmental operations, people take mental shortcuts in drawing inferences from data. Unfortunately, several of these shortcuts have been found to sabotage the decision-making efforts of otherwise responsible people whom we would normally expect to exercise sound judgment.

Maintaining Sound Process Judgment

Managing group processes is so important to the overall problem-solving process that the last third of this book is devoted to the subject. Chapters 9 through 12 deal with the rather complicated issue of how to design and manage teams to enhance the effectiveness of problem solving within organizations.

The focus of this chapter is more on the judgment required by problem solvers when dealing with the content of the problem rather than the process. Thus, we examine here the two areas of judgment that are more related to content than to process. The first area deals with conditions that cause problem solvers either to consider or not to consider certain information. The second deals with thought processes that affect the problem solver's judgment once certain information is taken into consideration.

Conditions That Start Judgment

Very few people take *all* the relevant data into account when they solve problems. The reasons for sloppy data gathering vary. A favorite excuse is lack of time: "We were under too much pressure to look at everything." Other reasons range from ignorance ("I didn't know enough about the problem to know *what* to look for"), to incompetence ("I didn't know *how* to find it out"), to lack of focus or direction ("We weren't sure *where* to look"). Of course, responsible managers are much less likely to succumb to these excuses.

But what about those people who are responsible but whose judgment still causes them to miss or—worse yet—to ignore critical bits of information? Several factors affect the judgment of managers in this context.

First among these is a personal predilection that competes with or prevents an appropriate situational analysis. Quite frequently an individual's decision-making judgment is based on certain powerful factors he is most comfortable with. In a study of managers from around the world conducted by Dr. Alan Rowe of the University of Southern California Graduate School of Business Administration, he determined that these powerful factors affect judgment in very visible ways.

The research revealed that although many factors influence decisions when personal considerations are involved, usually a single factor emerges that tends to be given an inordinate amount of influence and therefore dominates the selection. This tendency appears to become more pronounced the higher one goes in management, even though at higher levels of management more factors have to be taken into account when making decisions. When personal or behavioral decisions were involved, managers tended to revert to a single powerful factor based on personal preference, regardless of how detailed the analysis and regardless of the number of factors examined.

Another factor affecting judgment as it relates to the use of data is the perception of risk, predictability, and uncertainty. Dr. Rowe found that although managers are aware that risks exist, they seldom make explicit estimates of the identifiable risks involved in their decisions. More typically, they choose between a limited number of alternatives, using lack of time as an excuse for not examining potential consequences in greater detail.

We think another issue plays on this. Most people don't know how to deal with data in a way that allows them to be comfortable in choosing a course of action based on what the data might indicate. Because they're not comfortable with predictions, risk, and uncertainty, they gain comfort by choosing a course of action that is familiar to them. This usually turns out to be a course of action that either worked for them in the past or meets a personal need in the present. In other words, comfort wins out over safety.

To avoid this rut, it is important to understand some things about probability and uncertainty and to learn to recognize when it is important to try to assess probable consequences. To emphasize this point, Dick Lyles tells a story about when he was an officer aboard a ship in the South China Sea. It received an SOS distress signal from a sinking Taiwanese merchant ship. The merchant ship sank before Dick's ship arrived on the scene, but they searched the area for survivors for several days. During their search they found an empty life raft, then an empty lifeboat, and, on the third day, a lifeboat with a single survivor. This man told the following story:

> The day after we set sail we encountered a heavy storm. Although we were loaded beyond the safety limits of the ship, we continued ahead. The storm got worse, with high winds and gigantic waves smashing over our ship. During the middle of the night we began taking on water faster than the pumps could expel it. Eventually, the water flooded the engine room so deeply that the pumps and engine could not work.
>
> The captain called the crew together and explained our predicament. We were sinking, drifting helplessly out of control, and the storm was bad and getting worse. He had sent the SOS but had no idea when help might arrive. He couldn't radio again because the power was completely gone. He gave orders to prepare to abandon ship. As he did so, a huge wave crashed along the side of the ship and tore the metal canister containing the inflatable life raft away. We watched as the raft inflated about twenty yards away and bobbed off like a cork, disappearing into the sea. This left us with two old wooden lifeboats and twenty-six crew members aboard. We started completing the chores for abandoning ship. When a lull in the storm came along, we cranked the first lifeboat out and began to lower it by hand. Just then a violent wave ripped down the side of the ship and stripped lifeboat, lines, and tackle away, tossing them into the sea. The lifeboat drifted slowly away.
>
> Our attention was drawn to the final lifeboat. Carefully, we began to lower it. Near the end of its descent, the ship heaved out of rhythm with the water, causing the boat to smack hard against the water. When the

ship then rose and the water lowered, the sudden yank on the after-line caused it to part, leaving only the forward line to connect the lifeboat to the ship. Soon the lifeboat began to batter against the side of the ship, trailing on its short lowering line. Rather than see the boat reduced to splinters, the captain decided to cut it loose.

In the few moments it lay close beside the ship, panic set in. Each crew member was faced with a decision. Should he jump overboard and try to reach the lifeboat, which would surely not sink, or stay with the much larger but slowly sinking ship, hoping she would stay afloat until help arrived? Finally, I jumped. I struggled through the water and barely made it to the lifeboat. I shouted for others to try, but the distance had increased and they would not. About two hours later, from a distance of half a mile, I watched the ship sink with twenty-five souls aboard. Three days later, I was saved.

This story presents an interesting study in decision-making judgment. One man jumped, accepting an immediate risk and unknown consequences, while twenty-five did not. Obviously, at the time of the decision, all twenty-six thought they were making the correct judgment. Only days later, when the one was rescued, did the correctness of his decision become evident.

The question to ask is whether this could have been predicted in advance. Was there any way for any of the crew members to compute the probability of survival and thus quantify their decision in such a way as to give them a convincing course of action to pursue? Not in this case. Quantifiable probabilities are only relevant when the events being considered are going to occur fairly frequently and when all outcomes can be expressed quantitatively. (A coin toss is a good example. Each time you toss the coin, there are only two possibilities, heads or tails, and there is an equal chance that either will come up.) The case of the sailor and the lifeboat is different. The variables are *not* quantifiable, many are unknown (such as how near help might be), and the event is unique in the lives of those involved. Thus, this decision, like most management decisions, involves uncertainty.

Where uncertainty is involved, probability statistics and quantifications are of little help. And current research is showing that even in areas where statistics are available to help predict the outcomes of decisions and events, people tend to ignore them. Instead, people tend to react to such decisions in ways best known to themselves, ways that frequently involve mental shortcuts that channel judgment down the wrong path or bring the wrong criteria into play. These shortcuts are discussed in the next section of the chapter. Before examining them, however, it is helpful to understand a few more of the factors that frequently cause people to exclude data or to examine the wrong information when problem solving.

Factors Affecting Poor Judgment

• *Getting bogged down in tradition.* We've all been frustrated at one time or another when someone explains that the reason for doing something is because "That's the way we've always done it." Such statements certainly speak to one aspect of this affliction. But the far more dangerous aspect is when the tradition is so taken for granted that no one even thinks of challenging the assumptions that support it. A good way to counteract this tendency is to ask yourself on a regular basis, "Is this still the best way to do this?" or "How can things be done differently?" In other words, develop the habit of seeking alternatives as a matter of course.

• *Overcertainty.* This occurs when a person's reactions are dictated by what he "knows to be correct" rather than by what is most functional to the situation at hand. Often people pursue a course of action out of sheer bullheadedness, to prove they are right, rather than change their assumptions about the way things really are. The best way to counteract this tendency is to instill the attitude that every situation is different and that times change, so there is no "one best way" to do things that applies in all situations.

• *Reluctance to experiment.* Some adults, particularly business and professional people, get locked into very rigid, superficially rational, unemotional behavior and thought patterns. In contrast, many truly creative scientists, writers, artists, and managers describe their work activities as games and challenges. They enjoy actively experimenting with their roles, styles, and ways of thinking and doing, which forces their judgment to be tested in a multitude of different situations.

- *Low tolerance for ambiguity.* At times, responsible managers put up with ambiguity when they find it necessary to pursue a line of thinking or course of action that is relatively unclear. There may be a sense of movement without a clear sense of either direction or outcome.

- *Two-valued thinking.* This type of thinking results when people limit the range of options to a finite number of alternatives, totally excluding all others. The worst case occurs when the number of options is limited to two, which are diametrically opposed, and the entire range of options on the continuum in between is ignored.

- *Fear of taking risks.* Although fear of failure is a part of this, it is also important to note that judgment—as well as progress—is often stymied by the simple fear of trying something new and different just because it *is* new and different and the final outcome is speculative at best. If given a choice between doing something we're used to (and also has a reasonably predictable outcome) and doing something new and different, most of us will tend to pursue the familiar because it is less of a risk.

- *Lack of emotional involvement.* In our "rational" world, many people believe that: (1) emotions must be totally controlled if people are to work together as a group; (2) displaying emotion is a sign of immaturity; (3) the show of emotions blocks clear and effective thinking; (4) emotional expressions devalue the person to whom they are directed; and (5) people who show emotions have little concern for the feelings of others. However, most truly great accomplishments emanate from people who have passion. Properly directed passion is necessary to optimize both judgment and responsibility. Emotional involvement naturally generates energy and intellectual excitement that can be very productive in tapping into people's full potential.

• *Missing the interrelationships of data.* Data are irrelevant unless a specific relationship to a problem can be delineated. Data reported under one set of circumstances or in groupings with other data might imply one interpretation. Reported with another set of data, though, they might imply no problem at all or a completely different interpretation. When defining problems, take care that the data upon which you base your findings are interpreted in the proper context. More important, be alert to whatever interrelationships between data may exist.

• *Limited perspective and/or awareness.* Closely tied to the issue of interrelationships between data is the issue of perspective and overall awareness. Awareness includes both self-awareness and awareness of our surroundings. Perspective deals with point of view and the completeness of understanding one achieves regarding the relationship of self to situation. The more a manager maintains a broad awareness and a relevant perspective, the better she will be able to exercise sound judgment. This is also true for everyone in the organization.

Getting all the right information "into the loop" is only half the challenge in fostering good judgment within an organization. An equally important challenge lies in seeing to it that, once considered, the data are interpreted and evaluated properly and correct conclusions drawn from them that will lead to optimal decisions.

Thought Processes That Affect Judgment

Mistakes in judgment most often result from an overreliance on intuition. In the ever more technical and complicated realm of management, managers must be able to draw reliable and correct inferences from the available data in order to make sound decisions. As previously stated, most managers learn to use mental shortcuts. And while these shortcuts can be extremely useful—and sometimes even necessary—in solving problems, they can also lead to disaster.

The four mental shortcuts that most often negatively affect

management decisions are called *framing, co-variation, availability,* and *representativeness.* The following sections explain how each can work for or against responsible judgment.

Framing

The way in which information is presented creates a context within which it is interpreted, so that the context rather than the data is more likely to influence one's conclusion. Here's an example.

> A retailer with seven stores is considering expansion. The company can add stores in new adjoining territories, it can add space to existing locations, or it can add new stores within the current territories of its existing stores. Which strategy should management choose?

This dilemma is typical of those faced by many managers today in that it is complicated and has many variables. What's important to realize, however, is that the relative weight given to these different variables will lead the decision in certain directions. Assume that management was presented with the following:

> Our decision to expand has been narrowed to two opportunities: an acquisition of a competitor's store within our current territory, or opening a new store in a prize market area in an adjoining territory. The competitor's store is slightly overpriced, but servicing it would cost less since it is within the boundaries of our current distribution system, and we would have greater leverage with our advertising dollars. Recently, this store has been making steady inroads into our market share.
> The new store would be designed to meet the standards of our most recent store, which is the most successful and profitable store in the chain. The new market area is much stronger and has greater potential than our existing one. The price of the site is under

market. However, the competition in this new market will be much heavier, and the ramp-up costs will be greater, thereby increasing the overall risk.

Which should management choose?

The correct answer, of course, depends on the actual numbers, the company's financial position, and what goals it has set. But the outcome might very likely be more dependent on how the decision makers frame the issue in terms of risk and reward. If they are risk-averse, they will choose the first option: They'll stop their losses, turning them to their own advantage, and put less of their capital at risk by investing in a proven venture. If they care less about risk and choose to focus more on overall gain, they are more likely to choose the second option. The important point to realize here is that in either case, management could very well make a decision that is not the best for the company in the long run.

Perhaps the most important issue relative to framing, however, is the extent to which an organization's hierarchy of purpose (mission, goals, and values) provides the basis for decision making. If decisions are made and problems solved in the context of the organization's purpose, the organization will be more effective and successful (and therefore more responsible) than if they are not.

Decision makers will decide on the basis of prevailing values. If the prevailing values are also the stated values, the organization will be effective over time in achieving its purpose. If there is one common thread that permeates the writings of all modern-day management theorists, it is that values are one of the most important conceptual frameworks through which management decisions must pass in order for them to be effective. If the right values are specified and acted upon, they will serve almost as "superordinate" goals that drive the organization to a successful future. If the wrong values define the decision makers' framework, the organization will almost certainly falter.

Co-Variation

The principle of co-variation has a negative impact on decisions in one of two ways: (1) when a cause-and-effect relationship between events is implied although none exists, or (2) when a cause-and-effect relationship between two or more events exists but is missed.

Both of these phenomena happen in management more often than most of us would care to admit. Consider the two following situations:

> A mid-level manager is given the responsibility for producing project results, but not the authority. She doesn't have any control over the people from other departments assigned to carry out certain tasks on the project. When results fall short of the project goals, her superiors conclude that it's because of her inability to supervise—in short, that it's a people problem—when in fact they inadvertently set her up to fail by not giving her the requisite authority. Because they attribute the poor result to the wrong cause, they only create more problems.

> A company loses significant market share because of poor service and problems with quality control. Without gathering sufficient information, the managers conclude that the reason they are losing customers is because there is a new competitor in the market who is charging lower prices. They lower their prices without fixing the quality and service problem, thereby exacerbating their own problem, and creating a situation from which they can't recover.

Availability

Availability is described as the phenomenon that occurs when objects or events are judged as frequent or probable, or as infrequent or improbable, depending on the readiness with which they come to mind.

One example is the executive who decides to invest large sums of money in a particular product because "my wife says she wouldn't consider buying anything else." The hundreds of thousands of customers who must buy the product in order for it to be successful may or may not have the same buying preferences as the executive's spouse. But the executive gives unwarranted weight to his wife's preference because he hears it firsthand and more often than he does the market research data that may be more reliable.

An oft-cited example of the availability factor involves U.S. congressional representatives. They hear mileage estimates from the Environmental Protection Agency that are based on valid research, and at the same time hear conflicting reports from a fellow legislator who relates a different experience with his personal car. The representatives choose to believe that their colleague's experience is more valid.

Representativeness

Representativeness occurs when an object, event, or idea is mentally assigned to one category rather than another (insofar as its principal feature represents another category). Stereotyping is the most common example of representativeness. Certain traits and characteristics are assigned to people because of certain other, unrelated traits or characteristics they may possess.

The higher one progresses up through the ranks of management, the more representativeness takes hold in general. We've all heard the saying "He can't see the forest for the trees." It means that this person is so focused on details, or his immediate area of responsibility, that he has lost sight of the big picture.

As people rise through the ranks of management, the opposite occurs. It becomes easier and easier to see the forest and lose sight of the trees. The executive sees part of the data and assumes that that portion is representative of the world as a whole.

Implications

There are two profound lessons to be learned from all we currently know about the application of judgment in problem solving and decision making. The first is that leaders play a crucial role in determining whether sound judgment will or will not be the foundation for problem-solving and decision-making efforts.

The second is that the more complicated and intricate problems and decisions are, the more they rely on sound judgment, and the type of sound judgment required is most likely to come from a combination of responsible management and team effort.

The Role of Leaders

In reflecting on the barriers to judgment mentioned previously, we must ask, "How do we inoculate ourselves against these afflictions?" One way is to make sure that your problem-solving efforts are led by bright, verbal, and outspoken leaders. Responsible managers ensure responsible problem-solving efforts by constantly probing, testing, and questioning.

Throughout his life, Albert Einstein was plagued by people asking him to reveal the source of his genius. He once explained that he was certain his traits weren't inherited and went on to say, "Curiosity, obsession, and dogged endurance combined with self-critique have brought me my ideas." Every effective leader and all responsible managers possess these four characteristics to a large degree.

But then it's reasonable to ask, if one of the responsible manager's roles is leadership, how does he develop better judgment in others? After all, it's not responsible to be the only one in the organization to exercise good judgment.

It's at this point that we must also recognize that bright, quick-thinking, verbal, and outgoing leaders may actually *impede* good judgment in organizations as much as they foster it. Here's an illustration of this point:

> Bob had founded a $50-million manufacturing company. Because Bob was the founder, he had a better perspective than anyone else in the company. Because he had been with the company forever, he had a broader base of experience than anyone else. And because it was his money that had paid the price of his education, all the lessons from his experience were near and dear to his thought processes and firmly embedded in his judgment.
>
> As a result, Bob exercised his judgment forcefully

and often. People brought Bob problems and he solved them quickly. They brought questions, he gave answers. Bob was bright, articulate, knowledgeable, enthusiastic, energetic, competent, wise, caring, observant, and dedicated. He was also a huge impediment to his organization. He held the organization back because he created dependencies. Bob's style was to decide everything himself. Everyone else's style was to let Bob do it.

In order to get people to exercise better judgment, you must ask people to exercise their judgment. There is no more powerful tool in this regard than to use what we call the six magic words: *"What would you suggest we do?"*

Many managers who try this get discouraged because in the short term they get what they consider to be "dumb" answers. They erroneously conclude that using the six magic words doesn't work. But this is the wrong conclusion.

Responsible managers are prepared to hear "dumb" responses when they ask, "What would you suggest we do?" They especially expect this when they first start asking. But one of the characteristics of responsible managers that makes them responsible is that they are prepared to deal with these effectively in a manner that allows for the growth of the subordinate and the strengthening of the organization.

What do they do? The best way to help people exercise better judgment, when they don't know what to do or how to do it, is to lead them through the problem-solving process. Ask questions that help them focus on the key elements they might be missing (for example, "What exactly is your objective?" or "Exactly how do you think your answer will address the problem and achieve our objective? Let's go back to the beginning and work this through"). The problem-solving methods presented in this book provide a solid framework within which responsible managers can offer coaching and training to help their subordinates become more responsible themselves. But first, the responsible manager must be prepared to help them. And second, the responsible manager must realize that the best way to help them is to lead them through the problem-solving process so they will both learn to be more effective and to develop better judgment.

The Importance of Teams

Teams, if they are properly designed and effectively led, will generally produce better solutions to complicated, multifaceted problems than individuals will.

The remainder of the book is devoted to understanding teams and how to make them work effectively.

9

The Rationale for Teams That Work

The efficiency of problem solving is often measured solely by the time and energy it takes to reach a solution.* In reality, though, finding a solution is only one aspect of the challenge, and often it is not the most difficult one. The real challenge is getting that solution implemented. Creating a solution without simultaneously grappling with implementation issues is an "ivory tower" approach. What can you do to make implementation easier and faster? You need to go through the process of proactively addressing implementation during the problem-defining and problem-solving phases. This provides input that modifies and refines the solution—and may even modify the definition of the problem.

Getting the Input to Improve Implementation

How do you find the right input to help design a solution that is easier to implement? The first step is to realize that those who can best identify a problem are not always the people who are best equipped to solve it. Second, those who can best solve a problem are frequently not the people who should be called

---

*Due to the overlapping nature of problem solving and decision making and our desire to reduce word clutter, the words *problem solving* and *solution* are here used interchangeably with *decision making* and *decision*.

upon at the implementation stage. And finally, those who can approve the solution may be an entirely different group of people from those who make the decision. In other words, the input required to take a problem from identification and definition through implementation will likely come from a varied group of individuals. In still other words, you need a team.

> Long ladders don't seem to have much to do with saving jet fuel. But when United Airlines brought together its pilots, ramp workers, and managers for the first time to brainstorm on the subject of fuel conservation, the answer was just that simple. The idea was to use electricity instead of jet fuel to power planes idling at the gates. But ramp workers couldn't plug cables into the aircraft because their ladders were often too short.
>
> "In the past, we would have sent out an edict and nothing would have changed," says Robert M. Sturtz, United's top fuel administrator. "We were finally able to extract what the real problem was." The taller ladders will save United $20 million a year.[1]

Having a business problem is a bit like having a jigsaw puzzle whose pieces are held by different people. To make matters more difficult, those who hold the pieces may not work together or even know one another! Many are not even aware that they are holding critical pieces to "your" puzzle. The more complex the problem is, the larger the number of people who are likely to hold pieces of the puzzle.

Unfortunately, being in charge of the puzzle does not mean that you have all the pieces required to solve it. And trying to solve the puzzle without all the pieces is frustrating and inefficient. Faced with this situation, the irresponsible manager attempts to solve the puzzle using the pieces he has in hand and those readily available and then says, "I've done my job." The responsible manager, in contrast, takes the time and effort to understand who holds the various pieces before attempting to put the puzzle together. This requires a certain amount of business literacy or knowledge of how the various components of the business, its markets, and its competitors interact to produce growth, profit, and value.

With this perspective, the responsible manager can then orchestrate a successful solution by bringing the puzzle piece holders together to solve the problem. This may be a short, one-time gathering in the hallway or an ongoing series of formal meetings. Team members may be permanent or temporary, that is, involved only when needed as the team progresses. In any case, a team has been formed to increase the likelihood of efficient problem solving and implementation.

Organizational Structures That Block Teamwork

When you attempt to design a responsible team, you may find that the structure of the organization presents barriers to getting the holders of the right puzzle pieces together. One barrier arises from the way organizations divide work into functional specialties such as departments or divisions. The other barrier stems from the way organizations layer work into hierarchies based on authority. Real-world problems (see the shaded area in Figure 9-1) cut across these artificial structural boundaries. In this example, billing errors for customized production are causing customer problems. To solve the problem, responsible problem solvers must also cut across the boundaries of departments and the layers of hierarchy. This means learning to manage in areas

Figure 9-1. The boundaries of the problem vs. structural boundaries.

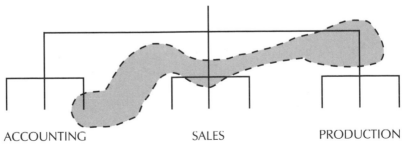

ACCOUNTING   SALES   PRODUCTION

where you do not officially have authority. Here is an example
in which the problem cut across departments, but the problem-
solving team did not.

> When one of the largest cities in the country decided to
> begin recycling in earnest, it elected to switch from
> using traditional trash collection trucks to the use of
> automated ones. The new trucks would use hydraulic
> arms to lift and dump trash barrels, which would re-
> duce the labor cost per truck and the frequent injuries
> to workers. The complexity of the recycling program
> and the new trucks led to the creation of a Department
> of Recycling, staffed exclusively by bright young engi-
> neers. They designed the new truck with a hydraulic
> arm on the right-hand side to lift and dump their spe-
> cially designed trash barrels.
>
> The engineers in Recycling asked Trash Collection to
> send over a few drivers to demonstrate the new trucks.
> Within minutes, the drivers had a question: "If the arm
> is on the right side, how do we pick up trash on the
> left-hand side of a one-way street?"
>
> The engineers did not want to admit an error, so they
> suggested driving down the one-way street the wrong
> way. The police would have none of that, so the engi-
> neers then suggested backing down the one-way streets
> while pointed in the wrong direction.

The truck design was an engineering marvel and an implementation failure. Trash Collection was not included in the
design, because the engineers decided the trash collection employees were too dumb to help design the new trucks. The ani-
mosity between departments escalated until consultants had to
be called in to help solve the problem the engineers had created
by not extending problem-solving responsibility across a functional boundary between two departments. This lack of respect
or appreciation for the value of the other puzzle piece holders'
input is a recurrent theme in problem-solving failures.

    In contrast, here is an example of a responsibly designed

team, one that cuts through the hierarchical barriers between workers and managers.

> A regional Coca-Cola™ bottler was concerned about the sloppy way its 350 delivery drivers were wearing the company uniform. In top management's eyes, the drivers presented a poor image to the community. A number of solutions were tried—memos, then rules, and finally disciplinary action. None seemed to have an effect on the workforce.
>
> A team was created that reached down through various levels to involve both drivers and managers. The drivers quickly identified problems with the uniform. One driver said, "I'm tall; my shirttail is too short. Every time I reach up to unload a case of Coke™, it pulls out. I think it's a waste of time to tuck it in 300 times a day!" Another driver said, "You give us lousy, thin jackets for the winter, so I wear my own. I don't want to get sick and miss work."
>
> And so it went, until the drivers had raised thirty-seven different issues that management had never considered. Eventually, the team designed new uniforms. When they arrived, the drivers on the problem-solving team stood by the entry door and announced to the other drivers as they arrived for work, "Here are the new and better uniforms that we designed for you guys. Wear 'em with pride." And they did.

When the organization's structure separates defining the problem, solving the problem, and implementation into three different activities done in different places by different people, it is very hard to get the desired results. But when people work together as a team and provide input and feedback, the entire organization benefits.

Organizational Cultures That Block Teamwork

These structural barriers are often reinforced by the managerial decision-making culture of a business. Not too long ago, management culture could be characterized as "Make a decision and then sell it." This approach, although focused on explaining and selling decisions instead of forcing them down people's throats, was essentially one-way communication. It enforced the belief that managers are responsible for identifying and solving problems while workers simply show up and implement their solutions—an excellent way to nurture irresponsible executives, managers, and workers.

> When top management at Sears made profit a priority, its middle managers responded by demanding that all Sears Auto Service Centers sell much more aggressively. Lower-level managers implemented this dictum by selling unneeded services to the consumer. The upshot was that consumers in turn brought Sears to court. Sears lost its quality Auto Service reputation and paid heavy fines. The Sears culture of top-down decision making nurtured irresponsible problem solving and decision making, which in turn led to disaster.[2]

The costs of poor implementation based on selling a solution to others has led to a more collaborative mode. This approach seeks input from the key puzzle piece holders much earlier in the process. Noted business writer Peter Senge characterizes collaboration as the process that produces the highest amount of energy and commitment to a solution.[3] (Note that collaboration always means consensus. This distinction is clarified in Chapter 11.) These two factors—energy and commitment—are critical to the efficiency and effectiveness of the implementation. Even when collaboration is not part of the day-to-day organizational culture, it can become the climate on a problem-solving team. This not only helps better solve the problem but also demonstrates the effectiveness of collaboration. This is the primary strategy that changes an organization's culture. A strong culture of collaboration is invariably based on high levels of mutual respect and honesty, which in turn build trust. Such a culture significantly reduces the structural barriers in an organization. Culture change is explained in depth in Chapter 12.

Teams as Remedies

Even though an organization's structure and culture may pose severe barriers to teamwork, it is possible to design responsible teams that cut across these barriers and operate with a new culture. In addition to successfully solving problems, such teams become powerful first steps in lowering the structural and cultural barriers.

The mechanism for integrating the defining of the problem, the solving of the problem, and the effective implementation of the solution is inclusion of the right people from the start. And inclusion means full participation in a two-way interchange that enables everyone to learn how to create a solution that solves the problem and is easily implementable. When done this way, the solution has value for all stakeholders because all were involved in creating it. The more significant the decision and the more complex the problem, the more likely it is that you need to include others.

Inclusion often looks like a team and inclusion will create a team, even though a team may not always produce inclusion. It is important not to expect teams per se to be a mechanism for efficient problem solving. Frequently, a team can be very active but neglect to notice whether the right people are on the team so that it can truly accomplish its task. Involvement requires constant awareness and adjustment of which people are needed and when.

When a team works on a problem, its members' understanding of the problem actually changes the nature of the problem. As the task evolves, some people may have to be added and others dropped from the team. Some may be needed only temporarily. A team with fixed membership cannot efficiently involve the necessary puzzle piece holders and may become another form of rigid structure with all the limitations of fixed boundaries. Inclusion demands a more responsive, flexible approach to who is on the team and for how long.

The Spectrum of Involvement

There are a variety of ways for more than one person to become involved in solving a problem. One way to look at this is by imagining a spectrum, with "telling" on one end and "collabo-ration" on the other (see Figure 9-2).

In telling, the boss makes announcements and shares information about decisions. Interaction is not desired or encouraged; the goal is compliance. In selling, the boss makes announcements with explanations of the features and benefits of the decision. Some interaction is encouraged to clarify issues but not to challenge them. The exploration of underlying assumptions or alternative solutions are outside the boundaries.

In consulting, the boss presents tentative or alternative decisions and seeks input to help in selecting or fine-tuning these decisions. The boundaries of what is fair game for discussion are pushed back, and participants interact much more freely. There is a sense of equality and there is honest and lively debate. The boss makes the actual decision and if the consulting process has been effective, all or most feel that it is their decision too. When intractable conflicts arise, the boss often steps in and switches to a telling style and makes the decision as an individual based on the authority of her position.

In collaborating, many can initiate, all participate, and all feel heard. There is an important switch from debating to dia-

Figure 9-2. The spectrum of involvement.

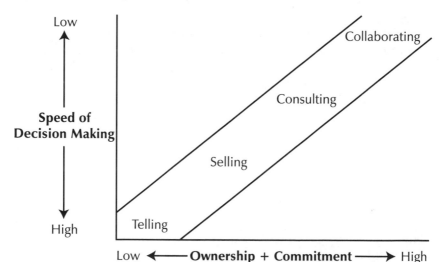

loguing, with less emphasis on selling your view to others and more focus on understanding the others' perspectives and challenging your own assumptions. The decision-making process in true collaboration approaches full consensus.

Each method of involving others has merits depending on the situation. The more complex the issue and the more change is involved, the more success there is on the collaborative end of the spectrum. The more routine and straightforward the issue is, the greater the likelihood that the telling end of the spectrum will be appropriate. Telling is also preferred when there isn't time to engage in a more collaborative method. (You can also combine methods, which is discussed later in the chapter.) Many leaders and employees are so accustomed to the telling and selling methods that they find it frustrating and inefficient to use a more collaborative approach without some structure. Chapter 12 suggests ways of doing this.

A skilled leader selects just the right amount of involvement for the issue at hand. One sign of an unskilled leader is always using the same involvement style regardless of its appropriateness. When you are unsure of the right level of involvement, you might favor the telling end of the spectrum because it is faster. You must then turn on your people radar and use the process skills covered in Chapter 11 to detect problems in commitment so that you can shift the involvement level toward collaboration in order to capture more commitment. An authentic leader—one who does what he says and says what he does—makes it clear which type of involvement is desired in each situation. This avoids appearing hypocritical—for example, by asking for collaboration while behaving in a telling/selling mode.

Three People Functions in Problem Solving

There are three different functions that people fill in making a decision or solving a problem:

1. Creating a solution or decision. People who do this are called the experts.

2. Authorizing the decision. These are the deciders.
3. Implementing the decision. These are the doers.

There are numerous situations each day in which one person fills all these functions. When the puzzle pieces of a problem are held by more than one person, these three functions are separated. Coordination and collaboration suffer since each function is populated by different people. Energy, ownership, and commitment tend to drop dramatically when the creators do not include the authorizers/deciders and the implementors/doers.

By combining the Spectrum of Involvement (Figure 9-2) with the three functions people fill when problem solving, we can get a clearer picture of how to create the needed ownership and commitment for high-speed, successful implementation (Figure 9-3). Collaboration at the front end during the creating of the decision ensures ownership at the end, where implementation occurs. Postponing inclusion until the decision is created and authorized reduces collaboration during implementation.

The function of authorizing a decision is usually filled by one person to maintain clear accountability and to support the hierarchical structure. In reality, a collaboratively created decision is very likely to produce consensus in the authorizing function. Thus this function becomes a minor formality between creation and implementation. However, if consensus cannot be

Figure 9-3. The "telling" mode vs. the collaborative mode in all stages of decision making.

THE THREE STAGES IN ALL DECISIONS

Creating	*Authorizing*	*Implementing*
I Create (Telling)	I Decide (Telling)	You Implement (Telling)
We Create (Collaborating)	I Decide (Consulting)	You Implement (Collaborating)

reached, keeping the authorizing function with an individual allows for a decision to be made without the organization being held hostage to those not agreeing. There is more on decision making in teams in Chapter 11 under the section on seven process tools.

When to Use Teams and When Not to Use Them

You should use a team only when it is necessary to do so, not because it's nice. During the last decade or two, the concept of participation in the workplace has become an end in itself. Too many teams, accomplishing too little and costing too much, were launched. In an organization, participation must be a means to accomplishing the organization's ends.

Teams get a bad reputation when they are created unnecessarily. You can avoid doing this by answering three questions before you create or join a team:

1. *Can an individual with the necessary authority make a good decision or create a good solution?* This means one that others in the field would evaluate as a "competent decision."

2. *If an individual makes the decision, will it be well implemented?* A well-implemented solution means that it accomplishes the desired objectives and removes the causes that created the problem. It creates no serious, undesirable side effects; occurs in the expected time frame; stays within budget; and does not require extensive policing or supervision.

3. *Is there time to have a team?* Inclusion takes time, and the issue may be so urgent that there is no time for a team effort.

A decision tree combining these three questions with their possible answers and outcomes is shown in Figure 9-4. These questions are a reflection of what responsible managers actually do.

Guidelines for When to Use a Team

- When one person does not have the information or experience to make a good decision, include the experts.

Figure 9-4. The three questions that decide whether an individual or a team is needed.

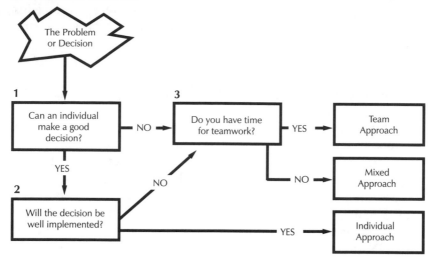

- When one person does not have the authority to make the decision, include the deciders.
- When others are needed to implement the decision, and they are not likely to be enthusiastic, wholehearted supporters of the decision, include those whose commitment is necessary.
- When the decision is likely to have a negative impact on others who have the power to disrupt the implementation, use a team that includes those who will be most affected or disruptive. As uncomfortable as this may be, it is the correct strategy.

Each of these four guidelines assumes that you have some appreciation of how others are likely to respond to your decision. Without some rudimentary people radar, you are likely to inaccurately estimate their viewpoint and reaction. Without some basic business literacy, you will not be sure whom to scan with this radar. Both these problems lead to forming teams when they are not needed, and to not forming them when they are.

Whenever a decision is not well implemented, you can assume that there was a lack of the people necessary for creating, authorizing, or implementing. To improve the implementation, include the missing people. Not including them at first may create a trust deficit that you will have to overcome.

Guidelines for When Not to Use a Team

• *You do not need a team when you have the knowledge and experience to make a good decision, when you have sufficient authority to authorize it, and when there is little likelihood that others will not be enthusiastic supporters of the implementation.*

• *Do not use a team when there is no time to include people in teamwork.* Take individual action and then use the mixed strategy described in the next section.

• *When you have made up your mind and are not open to changing it, do not create a team.* If a team *is* formed, team members will quickly realize that they are being manipulated to simply rubber-stamp a previously made decision. Their backlash will diminish your power and undermine the decision. Be straightforward and avoid hypocrisy. Announce your decision and that it is not open to change. Even when others do not like it, they will be more apt to support it when you are honest.

• *Do not create a team for a task that by its very nature is best done by an individual.* Editing the employee handbook is a good example. Using a single editor produces a consistent style of writing, so having one person do the editing makes sense. On the other hand, you may want a number of people to review the handbook and to suggest changes and a team to give it final approval.

Using a Mixed Strategy

When you feel you really need help in the decision-making process but there is no time, consider using a mixed strategy. This means that you begin with one strategy—individual work—and follow through with another strategy—teamwork.

The dispatcher of 100 dairy product delivery trucks realized that he would have to act fast when some thirty-
five of his trucks were made inaccessible by a flood. He
reassigned routes so that all deliveries could be made
using only sixty-five trucks. He doubled up some drivers to speed deliveries.

When the drivers reported for work, he knew that
they would not all like his plan, but he didn't have time
to sit down and have a meeting. He told them, "Due
to the flood, we are thirty-five trucks short. I've been
working since 4 A.M. to create a plan that might just
work if I have your support. I realize it's a dumb plan.
What I mean is that I'm sure if I sat down with some of
you, we could create a much better plan. But if we take
time to meet, we lose time to deliver. So I'm apologiz-
ing for my dumb plan and asking you to live with it for
today. At the end of the day I'll have some beer and
pretzels in the garage. As you finish your deliveries, I'd
sure appreciate your staying a bit and helping me plan
how we'll attack the problem tomorrow if the flood is
still here. What do you say?"

The support was unanimous. His humility in admitting
his plan was "dumb" gained the dispatcher control
over the situation.

Responsible Teams

The simplest definition of a responsible team is one that delivers
the right results. Responsible teams share certain characteristics.
They begin with a common purpose. This means that achieving
the goals of the team is important and meaningful to each team
member. Without a common purpose, teams founder and become frustrated. Invariably, the purpose is of significant value
to the larger organization.

The purpose is translated into specific, desired objectives.
These are measurable or assessable; in other words, you can tell
that they are being achieved and how thoroughly. The team

knows where it is going and has the navigational tools to measure its progress and to make midcourse corrections. These factors enable the team to hold itself accountable for its performance.

A responsible team is invariably made up of under a dozen people. Of course, the right people are on the team. Its members have the needed skills and knowledge. They may not always start with all the resources or authority to succeed, but they find and add these along the way. The team is learning, evolving, and improving bit by bit.

Finally, a responsible team is not undermined by its parent organization. At worst, it is simply neglected; at best, it is nurtured and supported.

Each of these key factors in responsible teams is addressed in the next three chapters. They lay out the concepts and skills for designing, leading, and supporting responsible teams— teams that deliver the right results.

Notes

1. "United We Are," *Business Week*, March 18, 1996.
2. "Sears Auto Service Backfires," *Business Week*, June 29, 1992.
3. Peter Senge et al., *The Fifth Discipline* (New York: Doubleday Currency, 1994).

10

The Design of Teams
That Work

It is one thing to believe that including the right people can improve problem solving; it is another to know specifically whom to involve to bring about this result. The goal is to involve the smallest number of people for the least amount of time who can integrate problem defining, solving, and implementation and deliver the right result. This chapter outlines a methodology for identifying which individuals are needed for a responsible team. It is based on an understanding of how decisions are controlled, not on how they should be controlled, not on how you might like them to be controlled, but on how they are actually controlled in the real world.

Controlling the Implementation of Decisions

There are three different ways of controlling the implementation of decisions.[1] They are represented by people who are deciders, experts, or doers. Although these roles often overlap, you need only ensure that a team has sufficient control over the creation and implementation of a decision.

Deciders have the authority to officially authorize the solution. Their authority generally comes from their job description or official title. Experts have the experience and knowledge to design a good solution. Because they can often control a decision by virtue of their expertise (and sometimes charisma), they have influence—the ability to affect a decision—even though they have no authority or power over the decision.

Doers have the energy and commitment to be personally responsible for the implementation. Often, the power that doers have is not considered in decision making and problem solving. But it is their power that often determines whether solutions are blocked or easily implemented.

Too often, the deciders make a decision without considering those who have the power to support or block the solution. After the decision is made, you often hear the deciders trying to figure out how to get the doers' buy-in. Replacing the concept of buy-in with that of involvement would ensure that decisions were better and more easily implemented. Not including the doers in a decision that will affect them is likely to undermine their support. One worker said that not being included in a decision that affected him felt like an overt act of hostility on management's part. People deeply resent not having input in the decisions that have an impact on their lives. Conversely, having input builds strong commitment to the decisions.

> A large southwestern city was designing a new city hall. The floor plans were put up in the employee cafeteria, along with red pencils and small signs encouraging comments. One barely legible response was from the janitor: "No slop closet on the third floor." The architect added one.

> What would the janitor have done if it had been left out? Knowing that no one would listen to him, he could simply have taken his mop and water-filled buckets up and down the elevator, spilling water and aggravating everyone to get his message across.

Power can be defined as the ability to give or withhold support and energy for a decision. Sabotaging a solution by exercising your power shows your displeasure, but it gives little information on how to improve the solution. Involving those with power in the decision-making process enables the doers to influence the solution constructively and to build true ownership in a decision. In this way, the decision-making process incorporates the design of the implementation instead of implementation being an afterthought.

Remember, the doers' power is always heard from eventually, even if they are not listened to. For example, your customers exercise their power when they choose to purchase or shun your products or services. You may not listen to them, but that does not prevent them from exercising their power to help or hurt your business.

Implementation and Involvement

As we have seen, decisions can be controlled by various combinations of authority, influence, and power. When decisions are largely made on the basis of authority, other people are involved in a telling or selling mode (as discussed in Chapter 9). As influence becomes the mode of control, involvement moves toward collaboration. The deciders often prefer not to be influenced by the doers, and they hope that the doers will simply obey their decisions.

Yet the doers—those with no authority and no channels to influence—still desire to have some control over their lives. Their only option is to use their power. This is often the source of unionism, resistance, and low motivation.

When those in authority open the channels of influence, those without authority set aside their power and depend on their influence to increase control over their lives. Paradoxically, as authority is replaced by mutual influence, everyone's degree of control in decision making or problem solving increases, as illustrated in Figure 10-1. As the figure also shows, responsible managers understand or learn who has what authority, power, and influence over a decision and its implementation. They then bring these people together to produce results.

The Relationship Between Authority and Responsibility

When individuals are assigned tasks, they often complain, "I can't do that. I don't have the authority, and if I don't have au-

Figure 10-1. The coalescence of three kinds of control in the over-lapping of authority, power, and influence to create greater control for all.

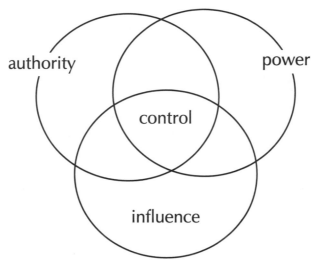

thority, you can't hold me responsible." This complaint is based on several assumptions, all false. The first is that simply having authority gives you enough control to make implementation happen.

The second is that if the organization were run correctly, everyone would have fairly complete authority over his assigned tasks. In fact, individuals should not and cannot have authority over all the areas they are responsible for. Remember, organizations exist to do work that is too large or complex for an individual to do. Even when the work is broken down into separate tasks or job responsibilities, the work itself cuts across these arbitrary distinctions. For example, launching a new product involves marketing, product design, production, warehousing, sales, delivery, and accounting. Who is responsible for the new product's success? Everyone, if you desire lasting success.

To avoid a situation in which no one feels accountable, begin with one person who is held accountable, even though she may not have control over the task or the team. That person can be held accountable for uniting the right people around the task.

Her work is getting every one to take 100 percent responsibility for the team's results. It's a bit like a successful marriage, in which each partner takes 100 percent responsibility. Relying on each person to take only 50 percent responsibility is a sure formula for an unsuccessful marriage—and an unsuccessful team.

Each functional specialty often feels as if it were not responsible for the whole success, but only for the part it has authority over. But if you gave complete responsibility to each functional area or department, it would balkanize the process and switch the focus to one of defending turf rather than solving problems.

The solution is that every person in the organization must take responsibility for the success of the project at hand, even if they do not have the authority. In order to exercise control in support of that responsibility, it becomes necessary to learn a new skill: how to achieve control by coalescing authority, power, and influence. Trying to control the results by using authority, or authorized power, invariably creates an energy-consuming struggle with the doers.

What is the ultimate answer to the statement that "I don't have enough authority." The answer is, "It is logically impossible to give you enough authority, and if you had it, it would not help you to fully control what you should be responsible for." There is no relationship between authority and responsibility. Organizations and leaders who attempt to manage complexity and change using only authority and power (that is, the traditional top down, command and control approach) frequently fail to address the full problem and inadvertently create additional problems. This is most easily seen when a problem cuts across departments and levels (see Figure 9-1).

Speeding new products to market has become increasingly important in our ultracompetitive world. Improving this speed is a problem that cuts across departments and levels. The primary strategy that has helped accelerate product development is uniting the right people across all the various departments involved in the new product. Marketing, research, engineering, production, sales, and distribution all become a cross-functional team focusing on the new product. When such a team truly coalesces the right people, the developmental process becomes parallel instead of serial. For example, pilot production runs are explored while the engineering is still in the design stage. This allows both pilot runs and engineering to cross-fertilize one another for a faster rate of learning. It also reduces the chances that engineering will finalize the design of a product that the pilot runs determine cannot be manufactured. Equally important, the individuals on such a team begin to take responsibility for the whole process of producing a new product, not just for their part in the process.

A responsible manager seeks control primarily through the use of influence skills in bringing together a variety of skills and by sharing information. Authority and power are rarely used or even implied. Both are held in reserve and used very, very sparingly.

The Design Process

This section zeroes in on the practical process of designing a team to make a decision, solve a problem, or improve a process. Every team is like a ballistic missile. It's going to blow up something, so it had better be guided.

You cannot design a responsible team unless you first know what its task or purpose is to be. Once the task is clear, you can decide who should be included so as to give the team the necessary control over the task. Launching a team without having a clear task in mind and without having the right members for that task creates an unguided missile that is likely to self-destruct, miss its target, or drift into oblivion. This occurs in many teams, committees, and task forces.

> A company president is concerned about the low motivation of many frontline employees. He puts together a team of senior executives and some workers to "take a look at the low motivation here and think about ways for improving morale." The team takes its work seriously and meets regularly for several months. Shortly before the team presents its recommendations to the president, he learns that the team has decided that a total restructuring of the organization is needed to

solve the low morale problem. This solution was motivated largely by the desire to move most of the team
members out from under a competent but very auto-
cratic operations manager.

The president now feels that he is in a bind. He has
made a commitment to support the team, but he knows
the team has come up with a very poor solution that
could affect profitability. Whatever he chooses to do
would now have a negative impact. Things would not
have come to this pass if he'd given the team a well-
defined task.

Defining the Team's Task

Let's focus on some specific ways to define a team's task. This
information is built on the seven-step method of problem solving introduced in Chapter 5. Note, though, that a task is not the
same as a problem. A task is a statement of work to be done.
When a task is delegated to a team or an individual, it becomes
an assignment of work to be done. A solid task description is the
basis of an effective handoff in launching a team or an individual
assignment. A poorly defined task allows a team to run out of
control, while an overly defined task can limit the team's ability
to define the real causes or create a good solution that can also
be well implemented.

Seven elements define a task, especially one that is assigned
to a team. The seven steps of problem solving are used as a
guide in defining the first four elements, which are of critical
importance, while the remaining three elements round out the
picture.

Element 1: Spell Out the Symptoms

These are usually the obvious events that triggered a response, such as a drop in sales, flat profits, declining morale,
increasing competition, or customer complaints. As was pointed
out in Chapter 6, simply listing the symptom does not define the

problem. The symptoms are clues prompting further examination.

Element 2: Spell Out the Causes

A problem definition means that you have identified the causes of the symptoms or the barriers preventing you from achieving the desired results. Defining a task at this level takes you much deeper than simply listing the symptoms. However, quite often, the causes are not known, and this element is delegated to the team.

Element 3: Set the Objectives

Determine what results are desired once the task is completed. (Review Chapter 6 to consider the four different types of results that could be set.) Not specifying the results opens the door to an activity-focused team that cannot and does not take responsibility for results but only for completing its activities.

Defining the objectives well requires that you have first defined the problem well. The work now left for the task is to find the solution that removes the causes or barriers and achieves the objectives.

Element 4: Spell Out the Constraints

What are the obvious areas that are off-limits? Constraints must be spelled out or the team can get out of control.

A five-year-old walks into the kitchen holding a dripping garden hose. He proudly announces to his parents, "I just cleaned my room." He saw his father use the hose to clean the car earlier, and his mother had asked him to clean his room. Lack of obvious constraints led to a task that got out of control.

Your team members probably have more common sense than the five-year-old, but they still need constraints. Some common constraints are "Do not interfere with day-to-day operations" or "Do not look for solutions by changing the organization's mission, strategies, or reward system."

Element 5: Spell Out the Schedule

Scheduling is a small but critical aspect in defining a task. It includes spelling out when work on the task should begin and be finished. If finishing the task is not likely to produce the desired objectives for some time, also spell out when the objectives will be achieved.

If the task will require more than a month or if those working on it are new to this sort of task, it is helpful to identify milestones and place them on the schedule. This helps everyone to have the same expectations. In some cases, the team may have to dive into the task and achieve a better understanding of it before a realistic end point can be set.

If the date cannot be realistically set at the start, set a date by which the date will be set.

Element 6: Spell Out the Resources

Spell out what resources will or will not be available to those working on the task. Resources include money, equipment, and facilities. One of the most important resources for a team that will require considerable time from its members is the answer to the question "Who will do my job when I am on the team?"

Element 7: Follow Up

How will you determine if the desired results occurred? How will the task be evaluated? Who will do the evaluation? And when will it be done? Although all this occurs only after the team has completed its task, it is useful for the team to have this information at the start to guide its work toward a solution.

* * * * *

A team's task is unclear until all seven elements of the task description are specified. Knowing all seven helps in selecting the right people. However, you may not be able to define all seven elements until you get the right team. It is entirely possible to launch a team when the only statement of the task is "We've got a problem with sales—please get some people together to work on it." In this case the responsible manager completes the task definition as the team progresses in its work. As the task definition comes into better focus, the responsible manager also adjusts the makeup of the team as necessary.

Composing Teams That Work

Once the task is clear, you can design the initial team. A responsible team design identifies the right people, creates a team of the right size, and assigns team members roles.

There are many different types of tasks that can be given to teams. For the purposes of this discussion, the focus is on teams that are assigned a problem to solve, an issue to resolve, a decision to make, or a project to complete. In other words, these teams are creating something new, not simply attending to day-to-day operations in a team format.

Selecting the Right People

To create a team that has the potential for acting responsibly—one that can deliver the right results—you must see to it that it has control over defining, solving, and implementing. To select the right people, ask the following four questions:

1. *Who has the authority to make the decisions that will be needed to address the task?* This is usually one person, but it could require more than one in some cases. This person is the decider.

2. *Who has the experience, expertise, and information needed to help design a good solution to this problem?* These are the experts.

3. *Who will be involved in or affected by the implementation of the solution?* These are the doers. Their energy and commitment are necessary if the implementation is to succeed.

(If the answer to all three of these questions is the same

person, you don't need a team but should assign the task to that individual. If the answers are different people, you need a team and now have a fourth question to ask.

4. *Does the team require the coalescing skills of a facilitator to integrate the various viewpoints, ideas, and interests into a good solution or decision?* Do not involve people just because they are available, are good team players, have volunteered, or hold certain positions on the organizational chart. None of these necessarily build trust and respect or have the ability to efficiently coalesce decider, experts, and doers.

Now take your list of potential team members and fine-tune it by asking these six questions about the team as it now stands:

1. Do you have the right team for a good decision?
2. Do you have the right team for good implementation?
3. If this team agrees on a solution, would others trust its solution?
4. Can anyone stop this team from completing its task?
5. If so, are these the "champions" who will drive toward high-quality results and effective implementation?
6. Is anyone so overcommitted on other teams that the team thereby becomes unreasonable? In general, no one should be on more than two task teams—and ideally, only on one team at a time.

Depending on your answers to these questions, explore adding people to the team.

Determining the Right Size

The size of the team must be balanced against its potential for efficiency, effectiveness, and the value of the task to the organization. A team may become too large to justify the time and effort needed to facilitate it successfully. Follow these five guidelines to determine how large to make your team:

1. Five to seven people is the ideal number. It provides for multiple viewpoints but is small enough so that each member can be a full and active participant.

2. Up to ten or twelve people works well but generally requires good facilitation for the team to stay focused and to ensure input from all.

3. More than twelve people is unwieldy but possible with expert facilitation.

4. If the team is too large, consider splitting up the task or breaking it into a sequence of tasks so that each step requires fewer people. Another possibility is to split the task into several smaller ones and to have sufficient overlap among the teams so that no team gets left behind.

5. If someone is not needed on the team full-time, use temporary membership, but be careful to maintain a core team with sufficient mass and balance of authority, power, and influence. Pay particular attention to maintaining two-way communication with temporary members. Having the decider be a temporary member is a sure way to add special challenges to the team. Regular two-way communication is needed so that neither the decider nor the team is left behind. The same challenges will exist in the implementation phase if the doers are not on the team.

Team Roles

A team generally needs defined leadership. However, the task of leading a team can be daunting. There are really several different functions combined in the role of "team leader." Because of the complexity of the task and because of the leader's skills or style, the leader often focuses on one of the roles to the exclusion of the others. Therefore, we highly recommend breaking out the various leadership roles. The more difficult, complex, or sensitive the task, the more benefit there is in having a skilled facilitator, in separating the leader or decider and facilitator roles, and in having a designated administrator.

The larger the team and the more difficult the task is, the more need there is for role structure. When you add structured roles, you improve the efficiency and effectiveness of the team. (This relationship is reversed with highly skilled teams, but these are rare.) Structured roles help ensure that the real issues surface and are integrated into the solution. Another benefit of using a formal structure is that it is one of the most effective methods for developing managers and changing the organization's culture.

A structured team has defined roles and follows a defined process with a defined team climate. Consider the following guidelines when evaluating the need for structure:

1. Teams of two to four people usually do not require formal roles unless conflict is high and members have little skill in harnessing it.
2. Teams of four to seven people benefit from a formal role structure, especially if members have not previously worked together as a team and/or the task is difficult.
3. Teams of seven or more people usually require a formal structure in order to achieve efficiency and effectiveness.

The four basic roles needed on most teams are:

1. *Decider*. This is the person who has the authority to make the final decision. The decider is on the team to learn from the others who will help her to understand the problem and to design a good solution. But the decider still has the overall responsibility for the decision and will have to "wear" that decision once it is made. Deciders can't always get to meetings since they are involved in so many things. Therefore, the decider must delegate, giving someone else on the team the right to decide without checking back with her.

2. *Facilitator*. This person's job is to design and lead the team process. This means maintaining a learning climate while leading the team through the seven steps. In addition, the facilitator keeps the pace moving, helps the team stay on task, and ultimately ensures that everyone is united around a good decision within the given time frame. This person has to be respected by the decider and able to manage any members who might attempt to dominate the team. The facilitator plans the agendas, helps coordinate the logistics, and conducts the warm-up and cool-down (see Chapter 11).

3. *Administrator.* This person assists the decider and facilitator in planning sessions, ensures that people get to the meetings with the proper preparation and materials, and makes sure that the environment is conducive to the task and that action items and decisions are recorded and communicated. The administrator briefs new members or visitors, sets up the room, posts any necessary charts, supervises the keeping of minutes, and monitors attendance. The administrator also keeps the facilitator informed as to the need for breaks or the time to end the session.

4. *Resource.* Everyone on the team is a resource. Members are there for what they know and what they can contribute. Their job is to be responsible to the assigned task and to be open, honest, and productive team members.

As the team gains experience and learns to interact well, the roles can become less formal. In teams with high experience and skills, the formal roles can disappear when not needed and return when useful. They are assumed informally so that the best person fills the needed role for just the right amount of time.[2] The evolution from formality to informality of team roles is shown in Figure 10-2.

Figure 10-2. Evolution of formal team roles resulting from the team's competence in managing group interaction.

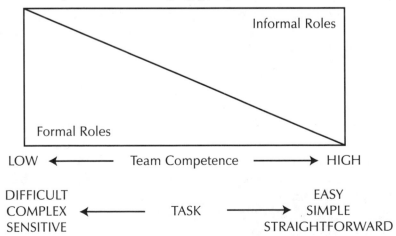

We are now able to define the team's task, design the team, and assign crucial roles to the members. Chapter 11 tells you how to facilitate the team so that it delivers the right results.

Factors Affecting Results

A responsible team can solve a problem or make a decision and have it implemented. This is a results team; it has been designed so that it can deliver the right results. It can go through all seven steps (see Figure 5-2) to implementation.

However, as an organization grows, the number of decisions to be made and problems to be solved also grows. Yet the number of deciders is still limited. There is not enough time for the decider to sit in on all the decisions that must be made. As a result, some decisions are not made or are made slowly and poorly. As this happens, the organization's ability to coalesce the right people declines. This slows down and decreases its ability to respond to competition and market changes, with the result that the organization ages and declines. The solution is decentralization and delegation.

A skilled facilitator can manage a deficiency of the right people on a team by intermittently involving the decider at crucial points and by keeping the decider well posted on team progress between meetings.

Some teams have so little authority that the most they can realistically hope to accomplish is to design a recommendation. This means that others not on the team will have to approve or bless the recommendation. This is a recommending team.

Too often, a team that is lacking a decider plows ahead to a solution only to find that it must now present its recommendations to the decider for final approval. Unfortunately, the person with authority usually chooses to revise, refine, or revisit the recommended solution. Invariably, the decider provides input that requires the team to backtrack or rethink its recommendation. This inefficiency causes team members to become frustrated (and not to volunteer for future teams). The impact on the team is demoralizing and deenergizing. This in turn nurtures irresponsibility among team members. In more than half the teams examined in a recent study, team members had surrendered and given up any real effort on the task.[3] Frequently, this individual loss of commitment is kept a secret from the team.

Many team members start out enthusiastically only to be jerked up short by the decider who reviews their recommendation by jotting across the page "You left out some critical input. I'm afraid you'll have to rework the recommendation." They started out trying to be responsible but ended up tired and discouraged.

If you are not able to give a problem-solving team full authority to decide on and implement the solution, be sure all team members understand the limits of their control, the form of their output, and the process for getting final approval. This is the responsible way of launching a team. On the other hand, if you really want to build resentment, let people think they are in charge and then kill their ideas after they have invested considerable time and energy in them.

Most executives recognize the value of and desire input from their teams so that they can build better answers to problems and have a workforce with greater commitment. But instead of acting responsibly, they work out the solution to a problem themselves and then announce it. In fact, they may even ask for feedback when they announce their solution or decision so that people will have a chance to have input. Unfortunately, by the time they've come to a conclusion, it is very difficult for anyone to give input. There is a strong predilection on the part of the creators of the decision to be subtly or openly defensive whenever their decision is challenged. The net result is no input plus a confirmation in the mind of the team that input was not really wanted in the first place.

The most effective way to create high commitment to a decision is to do it through high inclusion. This means involving all those who will be affected by the decision from the very start. Think of the problem-solving and decision-making process as riverbanks that begin very wide apart at the top and then narrow toward the output or decision at the bottom. At the very beginning, there is a great deal of unsorted information, data, opinions, concerns, and assumptions as those who are involved grapple with the problem/decision. As more data are accumulated, analyzed, and sorted, ideas arise and are explored, accepted, and rejected until the scope narrows down to an agreed-upon decision. This process may involve literally hundreds of microdecisions as you move down the river.

This river analogy explains why it is more difficult to build commitment from those who were not involved in the "funneling" process without backtracking and reexplaining or essentially redoing the whole narrowing-down process with the newcomers. Decision makers who are not sufficiently patient typically involve too few people. This makes it very difficult for those who were not involved from the beginning to raise questions with the same sense of confidence that was enjoyed by team members who actually took the issue down the river as it funneled to a decision point.

Thus, the later you involve people in the decision-making/problem-solving process, the less likely it is that they will be committed to implementing the solution and creating the desired results. The more change the decision encompasses, the more likely it is that commitment will be low from those not involved.

Model Teams

One way to address the high people demands of a responsible team made up of the right people is to limit the number of such teams. The right number would be just enough so that a critical mass of people in the organization—say, 20 percent to 35 percent—sit on at least one problem-solving or process improvement team a year. Having a few teams that perform incredibly well, whose members then spread the word, is more powerful than having an undisciplined proliferation of teamwork.

Changing Team Members

Since a team should be designed to do the task, the composition of the team must change if the task changes if it is going to remain responsible. In other words, adjust the team's members to keep the task and the team in balance (see Figure 10-3). Make sure that the team knows it is free to add or drop members if:

- The task changes.
- It turns out that someone is not needed for the team to be responsible.
- It turns out that someone else is needed to achieve the desired outcome.
- The team requires input from an expert.
- You learn of concern about or resistance to the team and the direction it is taking from those not on the team.

Figure 10-3. Adjusting the team's membership to balance the task as the task changes.

THE TEAM'S   THE TEAM'S
    TASK   CONTROL

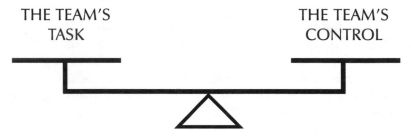

Notes

1. The concept that control is based on authority, power, and influence was articulated by Ichak Adizes in *How to Solve the Mismanagement Crisis* (Burr Ridge, Ill.: Dow Jones Irwin, 1979).
2. Jon Katzenbach and Douglas Smith, *The Wisdom of Teams* (Boston: Harvard Business School Press, 1993).
3. Reported by Professor Paul Mulvey at North Carolina State University, *USA Today*, February 26, 1997.

11

The Interaction of Teams That Work

Whenever two or more people come together to address a common problem, you have a team. Teams—even well-designed teams—in turn create their own set of problems. These are called process problems, as distinguished from content problems, which lie in the content of the task being addressed.

Every interaction between people includes these two distinct types of agendas. The content agenda or the topic discussed is the obvious one. You might call this the "what we did" agenda. The second one is the process agenda, the "how we did it" agenda. It covers a variety of significant factors that heavily affect the success of the team. The process agenda is intriguing because while everyone is aware of it, only rarely does anyone talk about it. It is like an underground current that determines how the meeting flows and where it goes. There are many interlocking elements in the process of a team. This chapter covers the basic elements of a responsible team's process of interaction.

When a team attempts to solve a problem and pays no attention to the process by which it does its work, each person contributes when and how he sees fit. Thus, numerous microdecisions are made by individuals as well as some by the whole group, decisions such as what to include, what not to include, how to analyze the situation, and so forth.

Inattention to the team's process of interaction results in a free-for-all approach to problem solving that may or may not produce a responsible result. In a responsible team, the process is structured for efficiency and effectiveness by beginning with a well-designed task with specific objectives plus a team of the right people. The seven steps are a map that structures the problem-solving process. The banks of the river, which contain the process, consist of the conditions for maintaining momentum, designated roles and responsibilities for the participants, plus specific conditions for how the team members interact in order to learn from each other. When the team has a strong, well-defined process, it is like a river with strong banks. The river flows fast and fairly straight. Without banks, the river loses energy and meanders. How process shapes and sequences the team's interaction is shown in Figure 11-1.

Managing the Process

Any team can improve dramatically when it pays attention to the process of its interactions. No special knowledge of team

Figure 11-1. The seven steps structuring a problem-solving process the way riverbanks channel the flow and speed of water.

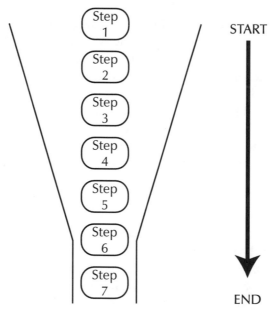

concepts or tools is necessary to do this. Simply stay conscious and notice what is happening on the team. Whenever the team is stuck or unproductive, look for what is causing this in the process arena, then explore ways to improve the process.

Most teams have enough collective wisdom to figure out how to address the process problems. However, there is tremendous reluctance to raising process issues. Some of this reluctance stems from a desire to be nice and not hurt anyone's feelings. Some of it stems from fear of speaking up because others may get angry. This reluctance severely undermines the effectiveness of organizations. Ultimately, this irresponsible behavior can bring an organization to its knees. Most team members have good process perceptions and practical ideas for improving the teams they are on. They just need to speak up!

The Process of Involvement

The value of involvement to building good decisions and commitment has been emphasized as a necessary step in making high-quality, easily implementable decisions. This does not happen simply by meeting together. A deeper synthesis is needed. The remainder of this chapter gives you the particular process technology for actually bringing together the holders of the puzzle pieces and for integrating their goals, experience, perspectives, and ideas to create quality solutions and commitment to implementation.

Coalescing a team's ideas and commitment is accomplished with the aid of the leader's charisma, plus interpersonal and group process skills. Underlying these is the ability to empathize, to put oneself in another's shoes and see the world from his perspective.

The quality of charisma has been described as the ability to make people feel better and stronger about themselves. This powerful effect captures peoples' commitment. However, charisma without expertise is dangerous. It creates high commitment to poor decisions. Even more devastating effects are produced when charisma is combined with narcissism (that is, a grandiose sense of self-importance, fantasies of unlimited success, and exhibitionistic behavior).

Modest charisma without narcissism, combined with strong group process skills, creates the ability to coalesce a team's ideas and commitment as the team moves from defining a problem to solving it, and then on to implementing it. When these abilities are combined with authority, the result is a very effective leader.

Even though charisma helps immensely in bringing together a team's ideas and commitment, it is still possible to accomplish much the same result without it. But you must understand the methods and skills of group process for building good solutions with commitment once the right people are in the room.

Many tough and persistent problems in organizations are unsolved because the right people have not been coalesced, not because no solution is possible. Training in problem solving and teamwork will not solve problems unless the right puzzle piece holders are present. In fact, what differentiates a good decision from a bad one is often more related to people's acceptance of personal responsibility for the decision, and their willingness to do whatever it takes to make the decision come out right, than it is to the specifics of the decision itself.

> Springfield Remanufacturing Corporation, which has increased its value 20,000 times in ten years, has developed quality products and customer service with impressive teamwork across the company. Yet almost no effort goes into training for quality, teamwork, or problem solving. The secret, according to CEO Jack Stack, is regularly opening the books to all employees, building strong business literacy among all employees encouraging employees to become problem solvers, and giving them a stake in the outcome. These four steps are a proven formula for designing an organization that can coalesce the right people with relative ease.[1]

Coalescing human energy in large corporations is very profitable. John Kotter's research on culture points out that of the 172 *Fortune* 500 companies he analyzed, the ones whose culture focused on listening to and responding to employees, owners, and customers were over 600 percent more profitable in a ten-year period than those whose culture focused on only one or two of these three constituencies.[2] Integrating the diverse needs of employees, shareowners, and customers means ideas and energy are coalesced.

If an energetic manager cannot coalesce people's ideas and commitment, she just works harder. If that is not enough, she then uses her power to force implementation. This tough approach may produce poor decisions and usually creates a backlash from the doers. It also creates inefficiency, which in turn requires implementing additional systems such as performance monitoring, rewards, and punishments.

Using authority and/or power to force a decision may have some initial success, but it backfires in the long run in that agreement was forced or sold. By contrast, using interpersonal and group process skills to exchange information and learn from one another may initially take more time and can produce conflict. This occurs when superficial agreement and being "nice" are set aside for openness and honesty. In the long run, this is the best route to truly coalescing the various control elements and building lasting commitment.

Dialogue: Uniting Ideas and People

Many of us use the word *dialogue* loosely to mean talking with one another. When you say, "We have an ongoing dialogue between the sales and production staff on how to better coordinate customer service," you probably mean that you discuss this in meetings, in planning sessions, and over coffee. But *dialogue* as we use the term is distinct from discussion. The process of dialogue deepens the inquiry so as to generate more information from which to fashion solutions that work well for all parties.

Dialogue is interaction between people of differing viewpoints with the intent to learn from one another. The purpose of this learning is to lay a foundation for creating new solutions to common problems. In discussion, the focus is on each party presenting, advocating, and selling his point of view to others.

The intent is winning or convincing others of your view. But dialogue cannot occur when one person believes that he has the "answer" and then focuses on selling, convincing, or educating the others.

In a dialogue, the primary sources of learning are the input of ideas from other people. As a result, the dialogue process functions effectively only in a climate of openness, collegiality, and mutual respect in which all are exploring one another's assumptions and viewpoints to better understand an issue. It is a switch from educating the other person to educating oneself.

Dialogue vs. Debate

There are two very distinct ways for people to interact in the "funnel" while they are engaged in the process of problem solving and decision making. One way is debating. The purpose of debating is to prove your point and to win. That very statement implies that the two debaters have come down separate decision-making funnels, arrived at separate conclusions, and are now engaged in a debate to prove which decision is right.

The debating process encourages bystanders to choose up sides. As the debate escalates, it can easily turn sarcastic or downright negative. A common strategy is to attack the other person rather than to explore the issue. This further heats up the emotional content of the debate and leads to great conflict. This might be called the polarization escalator, illustrated in Figure 11-2.

The debating process is often truncated within the hierarchical organization owing to the authority and potential power that those in the hierarchy hold. Debate rarely occurs in a boss-subordinate setting, which is based on the obedience of the subordinate. As a result, differences don't escalate into a debate in a hierarchical organization as easily as they might elsewhere. Those lower in the hierarchy go along to get along.

The process of debating has several serious faults. First, it tends to create a black-and-white view of the issue. Second, the process polarizes the issue, which does not allow for the synthesis of input and new data in an altogether different solution.

Figure 11-2. The escalation in emotional response to differences of opinion in the debate process.

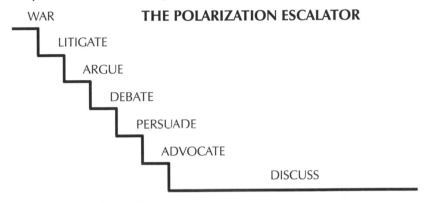

Third, the process tends to create a climate of antagonism that lingers, eroding the possibility of full commitment to the winner.

In dialogue, the goal is to create something new—a new understanding. The focus is on changing oneself through the process of exploring one's own perspective or viewpoint, particularly as differences surface. In other words, flexibility creeps in, and the distance between the viewpoints decreases as common ground is discovered. It is on this common ground of understanding that new solutions are built, typically with very high degrees of energy and commitment. Around the periphery of the common ground may lie unresolved differences, but the focus is not on trying to fight one's way through these. The focus is on the common ground. And as actions built in the common areas are taken and implemented, the unresolved conflicts often dissolve. When polarized sides realize that a decision must be made, they have no common ground on which to build a decision. Pieces of each viewpoint are glued together in a compromise that neither side really likes.

Figure 11-3 shows that when a difference arises, there are several decision points—A, B, and C—at which choices are made that determine the type of outcome that is likely. When a difference gets put on the table (point B), the participants begin to decide how much they want to win versus how much they

Figure 11-3. Three decision points at which it is determined whether differences will result in conflict, compromise, or dialogue.

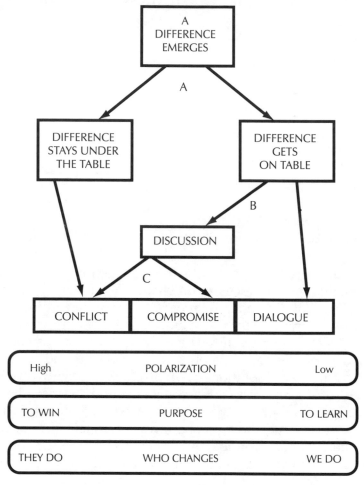

want to learn about the issue. If winning takes precedence over learning, the outcome polarizes the two sides and results in a full-scale conflict (point C). Quite often, the specter of such a conflict is enough to motivate the parties to compromise. But at this point in the process, it is much harder to move to a dialogue because the polarization must first be overcome. Notice that differences that do not get on the table still affect the outcome.

The Components of a Dialogue

It seems that people quite naturally and easily get onto the polarization escalator, which carries them to ever higher levels of disagreement and conflict. To stay off this escalator, you must make a conscious effort to do so. The alternative, dialogue, has the following components:

• *Inclusion.* Including the stakeholders is a prerequisite for dialogue. If all sides are not involved, this limits the size of the common ground that can be created, which in turn limits the options in creating decisions that will be valued by all stakeholders. The larger the circle, the better the solution will be.

• *Intention to learn.* Each person's intention to learn is the foundation of dialogue. Implicit in learning is making mistakes and accepting mistakes made by others.

• *Humility.* We cannot learn if we believe the other person or the other side is ignorant and if we do not perceive our own ignorance. It seems that the more formal education a person has, the more difficult it is to believe that those without an equivalent education can have anything to teach us. Paolo Freire, the Brazilian writer on change, said that true education is not A teaching B or A educating B, but rather A and B learning together.[3]

• *Mutual respect.* As humility appears, it becomes possible to respect the other person. From a practical point of view, this means that when we hear the other person say something that is not in agreement with our experience or view, we accept her viewpoint as valid. We don't discount or belittle her position. Instead, we try to understand how she has come to it. Dialogue is built on the concept of mutuality: You and I will learn together.

• *Honesty.* Honesty is the essential ingredient in dialogue, the *sine qua non* of all genuine communication. It is what allows us to understand our own basic assumptions about any issue and what encourages us to openly share our ideas and concerns, both facts and feelings, with others. Without honesty, teams and organizations can waste a lot of time and wind up stuck within the same old parameters of the same old problems.

• *Use of critical thinking.* Critical thinkers view reality as a continually changing process. Naive thinkers, by contrast, see the realities of the past and look upon the present as having emerged from that past in a linear, normalized, and well-behaved manner. The naive thinker wants the future to accommodate to the accustomed past. The critical thinker participates in the transformation of reality on behalf of creating a better future. Dialogue requires and fosters critical thinking. With it, you are creating new solutions, not trying to restore the past.

• *Willingness to challenge assumptions.* A critical characteristic of genuine dialogue is the identification and suspension of all assumptions. It is this process that allows new doors to be opened with a deeper understanding of the issues. However, suspending assumptions makes the dialogue inherently dangerous—dangerous because it can destabilize your worldview and force you or inspire you to see the world from a new and quite different perspective. Suspending assumptions is also difficult because it requires you to think through your assumptions instead of just accepting them as self-evident truths. Dialogue requires both courage and hard work.

• *Suspension of attachment.* Being open to a variety of outcomes and not attached to a particular solution makes it infinitely easier to involve others, to collaborate, and to learn. This does not mean that you cannot have strong views or favorite ideas. It means that you can and should suspend your attachment to them while engaged in a dialogue just as you temporarily suspended your assumptions.

• *Toleration of ambiguity.* A good dialogue takes you into unexplored territory. While there, ambiguity and uncertainty grow. In grappling with tough issues, the tendency for the team when it finds itself in the middle of nowhere is to give up or to jump to conclusions or to accept compromises prematurely.

Don't do it. This is where the creation of new solutions takes place.

• *Acknowledgment of the conflict.* A dialogue is not an exercise in diplomacy. Therefore it is counterproductive to try to smooth over differences and pretend they don't exist. In fact, it is necessary always to identify, acknowledge, and name the conflict, even to post it on the wall. But there should be a focus on the areas of agreement first. Use these conflicts to learn about the other person's view and ultimately about your own view. Use these new understandings to build common ground. If it turns out that there are insufficient resources for building effective solutions in these common ground areas, then move to the periphery to address the conflicts. With higher levels of mutual respect, the team can address higher levels of conflict productively.

• *Collaboration.* In a dialogue you are working *with* someone, not *against* him. You are neither the prosecuting attorney nor the attorney for the defense. Therefore, consciously avoid all advocating, competing, convincing, selling, telling, intimidating, and forcing. Only in this way can true collaboration be attained.

• *Allowance of time.* Learning how to participate in a dialogue and to use this process to advantage takes time, sometimes considerable time. But if you do not allow time to practice and develop it, dialogue will not happen. This would be a shame because an organization's investment in learning how to dialogue can provide almost immediate payoffs and give it a long-term advantage that competitors will find hard to duplicate.

Unless dialogue has become institutionalized, you may find your team under time pressure to reduce its collaborative efforts in order to produce a result—any result. Be honest with your team in this event. If time pressures take precedence, use a mixed strategy as described in Chapter 9. This allows you to respond to the time urgency without undermining your commitment to dialogue. Return to the dialogue at a later date.

As the organization invests time in building the conditions of dialogue, your ability to create energy and commitment will increase as a result of the more collaborative interaction between people.

Creation of a Dialogue-Friendly Climate

Whenever you are creating a new climate for a team or a new culture in an organization, people will be uncertain in their use of it. It is essential to regularly remind people of the desired climate for dialogue in meetings and quickly but respectfully to reprimand those who forget and switch back to the old climate. Most of all, it is essential to show people that the new climate is effective (it helps you to work on the task better) and safe (no one is going to be punished for using it). As its effectiveness and safety are demonstrated, team members will more thoroughly adopt the conditions for dialogue.

Diagnosis of Dialogue

Whenever a group elects to engage in a dialogue, it will invariably violate one or more of the conditions set out for its functioning. If there is no conscious identification of the violation, followed by corrective action, the dialogue will take a step closer to the process of debating. It takes only two or three such incidents that violate the conditions of dialogue to switch the process back into the debate mode.

When this occurs in a hierarchically structured organization, the dynamics of the culture tend to suppress any acknowledgment of the switch from dialogue to debate. People think that the boss wants to change the climate back to the old ways. It may appear on the surface that the team has come to agreement, when in fact it has come to compliance. It can be difficult to detect this subtle switch.

The following diagnostic procedure can keep your team from falling into this trap:

1. Make sure that everyone on the team is aware of the conditions that make dialogue possible.
2. Effective dialogue builds common ground, which increases the information available for good decision making. Look for greater trust, energy, and commitment as well as teamwork.

3. If you are not getting these results, you are not dialoguing. Try these options:
   - Review the conditions for dialogue. Identify the element(s) on which the team is weakest, and discuss how to strengthen the process.
   - Ensure that there is mutual respect.

The Seven Basic Process Tools

The following seven process tools will help your team avoid the common process problems that can get in the way of the team's work.

Warm-Up

Basketball players and ballet dancers need time to warm up. Not warming up limits the quality of their performance and increases the chance of injury. The same principles apply to human interaction. Warming up gets participants ready to do the work.

Every meeting benefits from a warm-up at the beginning and a cool-down at the end. The longer and more complex or sensitive or difficult the meeting is, the longer and more indepth the warm-up and cool-down should be. In task team terms, warming up (or getting ready) includes focusing on the task, connecting with the others on the team, disconnecting from distractions outside the team, agreeing on the rules of engagement, and making sure that everything and everybody you need are on hand.

Allow about 10 percent of the meeting time for warming up. At the first meeting of a task team containing people who are new to such a team, the warm-up may take the better part of an hour. Do not make it overly laborious, but be sure not to skip any key area. Assess the team's warm-up needs, and design the warm-up using the list of areas shown on page 196 as a resource. Not all warm-up areas have the same importance in every meeting; choose the key items to stress. The simplest warm-up asks,

"What are your thoughts and feelings as we begin to work on this task today?"

Here are areas to explore and confirm during the warm-up process:

- Clarify the team's task and today's agenda.
- Surface and dispel any distractions.
- See that the logistics are appropriate and supportive.
- Make sure that you have the right people for the task.
- Confirm that members are truly ready to work as a team.
- Set ground rules that the team agrees to follow.

The Seven-Steps Road Map

The seven steps for decision making and problem solving were thoroughly presented in Chapters 5 through 8. These steps provide a road map for any managerial or organizational problem, decision, or process you wish to work on. The seven steps tell you what the major thrust of the team's agenda should be for each meeting. To lead the meeting well, determine the answers to these questions:

- Which steps have we done?
- Have we left any steps out of the sequence?
- What step comes next, and how can we prepare for it?

Individual and Team Accumulation

This is a powerful technique, which can be used in any of the seven steps, for involving everyone on a team in looking at complex or sensitive issues. It increases openness, participation, and mutual respect while avoiding "group think." The process is divided into three elements:

1. *Defining the topic.* For example:
   - What are the key issues in a successful referral program?
   - What are the causes of delays in processing applications?

- What are your concerns about the new project?
2. *Individual accumulation.* Have members respond to the topic from their individual points of view:
   - Write an exhaustive list.
   - Write one item at a time. Do not link elements together in long cause-and-effect explanations.
   - Describe what is happening, not what the solution should be—for example, "Sales have been down for six months," as opposed to "We need to improve sales training."
   - Work individually and in silence. Do not distract others.
   - Be 100 percent honest. These notes are only for you.
3. *Team accumulation.* Have everyone share their input.
   - Go around the table in round-robin fashion. Each person gets a chance to speak, then calls the name of the person to her right when she is done.
   - Have each person mention only one item at a time so that the momentum keeps up and everyone participates.
   - Keep going around the room until everyone is "dry."
   - Do not allow discussion. It slows the process down and can undermine the climate.
   - Maintain mutual respect by allowing no discounting, commenting, or jokes.
   - Pause only to clarify a contribution.

Once all the input has been delivered, now is the time for the dialogue to begin. Individual and team accumulation is a time-consuming process. Use it sparingly, or abbreviate the formality.

Convergence and Divergence

As facilitator, you should always be aware of whether the process a team is engaged in is diverging or converging the team. Individual and team accumulation or brainstorming create divergence by adding more information and bringing to the surface more ideas and viewpoints. In contrast, focusing on categorizing objectives or setting priorities converges the team. It would therefore be unwise to follow individual and team accumulation with brainstorming since the team would enter into an information overload. The general rule of thumb is to alternate convergent and divergent activities unless you have a good reason for not following this pattern.

Pace and Focus

The facilitator must aggressively manage the pace and focus of the team.

The pace has to vary. When issues are straightforward, hurry the team along; do not allow dawdling. When it is time to go deeper into a complex or sensitive issue, slow down and take the time, but always stay on task.

Adhering to the purpose during the meeting means noticing when you are off target and steering the members back on course. You can help get the team back on the path with interventions such as:

- "I think we are getting off the subject."
- "Can someone tell me what we are trying to accomplish now?"
- "Help! I don't understand how this discussion relates to our purpose."
- "Mary, what are your thoughts on what we need to do to meet our goals?"

Beware of so rigidly adhering to the subject that intriguing sidetracks are aborted or opportunities for creativity are ignored.

Decision Making With Teams

Every problem-solving team must make decisions—major ones on such an issue as "Which solution will we select?" and minor ones such as "How long shall we meet today?"

Too often, those with the authority to make a decision are concerned that they will lose this right if a team is involved. A fundamental rule for responsible teamwork is that no actions of the team should in any way undermine the authority of the normal hierarchy without that hierarchy's approval. The purpose of the team is not to change the hierarchy. Thus, the person with authority to make the decision in a certain area retains that authority or right even when a team works in his area. The only difference is that the decider will now have more input from the team, and the team will have more input from the decider before the decision is made. This input may change the decider's views or the doers' views.

"Democraship"

"Democraship" is a way of making decisions on a team that combines the speed of strong leadership with commitment to a democratic consensus. It combines *democra*cy and leader*ship*. To see how these combine, you must distinguish three aspects in reaching a decision: creating, authorizing, and accepting.

The creating of the decision occurs in the dialogue that goes on among team members as they work through the seven steps. The team is fashioning, creating, or assembling a solution.

The authorizing of a decision occurs when the decider says, "This is the decision I will authorize." The decider has used the team as a medium for mutual learning to gain more ideas and perspectives so that he will authorize a better-informed decision. This mutual learning between the decider and other team members is at the heart of creating a decision that takes the concerns of the others into account. This process of cocreation captures each individual's commitment to the decision. The decider is an equal during the creating of the decision. But in the authorizing of the decision, the decider is first among equals. Only the decider can authorize the decision. He accepts full responsibility for the decision and its implementation. He is held accountable.

The acceptance of the decision by the team is tested during the cool-down. Acceptance will be extraordinarily high if the decision that was authorized was the result of a well-integrated decision-creating process. In this case everyone on the team is committed and takes responsibility for the decision. If it turns out that some significant number of the team members do not accept the decision that was authorized by the decider, then the process of creating the decision was poorly facilitated; that is, no mutual learning occurred.

Suppose We Still Do Not Agree?

Even with good facilitation, you may end up in the decision-making step with not everyone in 100 percent agreement. If the facilitation has been good, however, you should expect operational consensus.

Operational consensus sounds like this: "I understand what you want to do. I would not do it that way. I feel that you understand my view, and I feel that you have given me a fair chance to influence you, but I have not been able to do so. Therefore, as a member of this organization and a supporter of its purpose, I will enthusiastically support your decision, and I will not undermine it in any way."[4]

Voting

Voting should not be used to make decisions on task teams. It is a quick way to resolve differences, but it has severe drawbacks when you want a good solution with high commitment. Voting can stop the investigation into the problem or decision before it has been fully explored or resolved. Voting fails to really grapple with the issues through dialogue and learning and rushes for closure. Thus, the result may be a superficial response to symptoms.

In voting, the majority rules. This can mean that up to 49 percent of members are opposed. This polarization of the various viewpoints is not the way to create the common ground and commitment needed for good implementation.

Cool-Down

Cooling down gets the team ready to end the work in a productive way. Working right up to the time when people start walking out of the meeting means you have not cooled down. This means that there is a high likelihood that the task and many participants are "left hanging" or incomplete.

Before ending, allow time for everyone to review the meeting. This should take up about 10 percent of the total meeting time. People need some time to digest what has happened. New insights may require some reflection. Here are several key areas to consider reviewing during the cool-down:

• *Review any assignments and decisions that were made.* Confirm that each has delineated *what* will be accomplished, *when* it will be done, and *who* will be held accountable. At times you may need to spell out *how* it will be done.

• *Review any agenda items that should be carried forward to a future meeting.* Discard those that no one is interested in, and seek preparation assignments for those in which there is interest.

• *Scan the balance of team members versus the task.* Are the right people present? Decide if any additional stakeholders should be incorporated or updated on the team's work. Should anyone be dropped from the team because he is no longer needed?

• *Decide on future meeting dates, times, and places.* Be sure to schedule several meetings in advance.

• *Finally, evaluate today's meeting.* Review what progress was made; evaluate the team's morale, energy, commitment, and process; and clarify who or what helped or hindered and how you can do better the next time.

Determine what support or help is needed from the rest of the organization in order to complete the task successfully.

Disruptive Behavior

Overly negative, argumentative, and humorous behavior can disrupt a team's progress. The best way to handle such situations is to prevent them. At the beginning of the meeting, ask members to agree on ground rules, as, for example, no interrupting, listening to each person, maintaining honesty and mutual respect. Once participants have agreed to these rules, it is easier to enforce them. If you need extra backup, ask the team for permission to enforce the rules.

The Role of Conflict on Teams

Much conflict arises from the fact that different people hold different pieces of the puzzle. We need all the pieces to solve the puzzle. The differences in viewpoints and experience are to be treasured because it is in these interactions that creative solutions can emerge.

Too often, teamwork is seen as nice work or cooperation. In other words, we have good teamwork if we all agree and you do what I say. The challenge in bringing the different puzzle piece holders together is that they will be and should be in conflict. Dialogue fosters productive conflict, which allows us to redefine the problem. In contrast, unproductive conflict focuses on winning or promoting our favorite solution.

Conflict always occurs. Different people have different goals, styles, positions, training, and interests. The danger is when it is hidden or smoothed over. This makes it seem peaceful on the surface, but it is never peaceful below the surface. The conflict invariably exerts its influence in hidden and devious ways that can prevent us from interacting successfully.

Conflict is necessary. Only through conflict can we encourage differences to surface, test, and temper our decisions; to stimulate new ideas; and to capture energy. Conflict is a positive sign. It occurs in organizations when people act responsibly. They speak up because they are committed to the organization's goals. Conflict is inevitable and indispensable to good teamwork and good management. The problem is not the conflict—it's the process by which it's handled.

Ultimate Teams

Now that everyone on the team is practicing the desired conditions for dialogue, it is time to up the ante. Top-level teams in business, sports, and the theater are top-level because they are constantly thinking about the whole team, not just themselves in relation to the task. Thus, a characteristic of the highest-performing teams is not that each individual follows the conditions of dialogue, but that each team member is supporting and encouraging every other team member to use these conditions. When this happens, the culture matures at warp speed.

This process of intuitive collaboration occurs within a business when department heads know one another well enough so that when sales designs a new program it doesn't have to include the warehouse on the team even though the warehouse has tremendous power over the success of the program. Sales knows and understands the warehouse's side well enough, and respects it sufficiently, to design a program that takes the warehouse's needs, dynamics, and concerns into account. Sales does not say "Trust us" to the warehouse. The warehouse says "We trust you" to sales, because sales has demonstrated that it understands the warehouse's viewpoint and takes it into account when making decisions that affect the warehouse. When all this happens, the organization becomes truly interconnected and organic. Each person is conscious of the whole.

The efficiency of this sort of connection is extraordinary. This high level of teamwork without team meetings to discuss everything is relatively rare in business. It is common, however, in sports and in the arts. In fact, the best sports teams, dance troupes, and acting and musical groups would probably not be the best if this subtle blending of the hearts did not occur.

Good teamwork is a way of bringing the organization to life by enabling different parts of the organization to learn about other parts and to understand how these parts are mutually interdependent. With sufficiently good teamwork, over time an organization will see a reduction in meetings and an increase in each person's consciousness of other individuals, of other departments, and of the whole organism.

Notes

1. Jack Stack with Bo Burlingham, *The Great Game of Business* (New York: Doubleday, Currency, 1991) and personal communications during a plant visit in 1995.

2. John Kotter and James Heskett, *Corporate Culture and Performance* (New York: The Free Press, 1992).
3. Paulo Freire, *Pedagogy of the Oppressed* (New York: Seabury Press, 1968).
4. Operational consensus was first defined by Edgar Schein in *Process Consultation: Its Role in Organizational Development* (Reading, Mass.: Addison-Wesley, 1969).

12

Keeping Responsible Change Alive

One big reason for the failure of many change efforts in business today is the pressure for profits. Profits can be created in two fundamentally different ways. Constructive profit results from the creation of value for three sets of stakeholders: owners, customers, and employees—the triple bottom line. Destructive profit results from reducing costs by reducing value to one or more of the three sets of stakeholders. Many senior executives, most managers, and all financial reports are not able to distinguish between constructive profit and destructive profit. As a result, most corporations choose the easier and faster way: the creation of destructive profit by reducing costs. The pressure for profits focuses improvement efforts on cost cutting and relatively quick-fix, superficial changes.

Such change efforts are almost doomed to failure. The information available suggests that the failure rate of serious organizational change efforts is well over 50 percent. In 1991, *Business Week*, *Fortune*, and *Forbes* all reported on the failure of total quality management (TQM) to add value.[1] Of the forty companies lionized by Tom Peters in his business best-seller *In Search of Excellence*, only four continued to meet the original criteria of excellence a few years later.

When reengineering hit the streets in the early 1990s, it too was touted as the Holy Grail of change technologies. Yet reengineering gurus often quote a failure rate as high as 70 percent.[2] Meanwhile, the failure rate of mergers and acquisitions to add long-term value to owners is placed at about 85 percent by two separate studies in two different decades.

Don't let the failures stop you from changing. The payoffs can be enormous. A recent study by the National Institute for Science and Technology reports that the sixteen winners of the Malcolm Baldrige National Quality Award from 1988 to 1997 have outperformed the Standard & Poor 500 stock index by 300 percent.[3] Even the forty-eight runners-up saw a 200 percent better performance than the S & P 500.

Why Change Efforts Fail

Fundamentally, most change efforts fail because of an inadequate understanding of what produces value in the business or of how human beings change. Here are eight specific reasons why change efforts fail. These reasons often act in concert to reinforce one another.

1. *Change fails because we like to feel good.* The vast majority of organizational change is motivated by pain or fear of pain. When change starts and reduces the pain, we begin to feel better, and we thus lose the motivation to continue changing. The change effort has moved the organization from the status of "sick" to "not sick." "Not sick" means you feel good even though you are not truly healthy. To move to health, you still have to do a number of things that won't initially "feel good." And while the organization can comfortably rest here, it becomes less nimble. When change is again required, the organization is less able to change.

2. *Change fails without top leadership's support.* If top management does not enthusiastically participate and openly support an improvement program, the effort is doomed to failure. This truism is regularly neglected. Unless senior management is prepared to actively support and even head the change effort, the urgent demands of day-to-day activities will eventually overpower the rest of the organization's initial commitment to a sustained improvement effort.

3. *Change fails when it does not address the whole system.* All the flavors of the month of organizational improvement methods have some validity—some. But none address the whole system of an organization. And all will fail if other key changes do not take place. Change efforts must pay attention to the whole system. This does not mean that the whole system must change in order for any change to occur. But it does mean that the change effort must examine all parts of the organization to identify which areas should be redesigned to reduce barriers and create support for the designated change. Action without diagnosis of the whole system is mismanagement.

A classic example of neglecting the whole system is not paying attention to changing the corporate culture to support strategic changes. Many think that company culture is too nebulous a concept, too "touchy-feely," for respectable, hard-nosed businesspeople to attend to, yet it is the culture that is often the barrier to change. Even when culture is seen as a significant barrier to change, it is often given only token attention.

Thus the fast growth of an entrepreneurial business instills a culture of growth. Success is equated with growth. When the new business plan calls for increased profitability, the culture of growth can block all efforts at increased profit.

4. *Change fails because we hide failure.* Many system theorists point out how difficult it is to learn from a successful system. There may be hundreds of components in a well-run business— some critical, others not. How do you determine which is which? Watching a successful airplane flight does not reveal what needs to be improved in the plane's structure. Investigating a plane crash, however, can reveal that it is the rear engine mounting bolt that failed, and this in turn reveals precisely how to make the plane better. The analysis of failure is the most valuable mine of improvement ideas in any organization. Yet most often a business avoids examining its own failures and instead looks to another successful business as a guide to its own improvement efforts.

5. *Change fails because of misunderstanding of change.* Two critical characteristics of the process of human change are illustrated in the cycle of change depicted in Figure 12-1.[4] First,

Figure 12-1. The cycle of change.

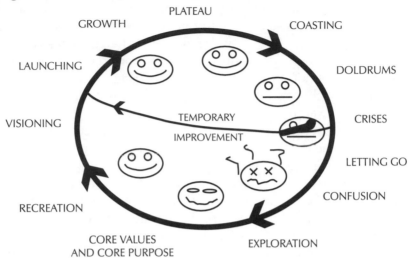

change occurs in a cycle, not in a linear fashion. Second, it proceeds in one direction; it does not go in reverse. In the beginning (visioning, launching, and growth), what we value and what we do are in sync.[5] But inevitably, they get out of sync. Either we change or the world changes. This brings the organization to a plateau.

At first this is enjoyable. But the resting that we enjoy on the plateau leads to coasting. Energy drops and happiness is transformed into mere satisfaction. Things are not good, but neither are they bad. As inevitable change continues, things get worse; doldrums turn into impending crises. But the marvel of the human mind prevents us from experiencing how bad things have gotten. We put on a blindfold and enter a state of denial.

Hard work may now become an effective analgesic for masking the pain of reality. Denial ends when the institution becomes collectively aware of the pain, which too often happens in a crisis.

We then enter the next stage—confusion. Here we can more clearly see how out of sync things are. It is this disintegration that lays the foundation for a creative reintegration and renewal. The change leader's role is to help the institution move through denial and through confusion. The institution must focus on its core values and purposes and create new ways.

6. *Change fails because too few know the rationale behind it.* While serious change must be initiated from the top, the rationale for changing often stays at the top. Others do not know why the change is needed. Thus the first step in leading change is to let those who must change understand why change is needed. Include them at the start, not at the tail end. Awareness and understanding of the reason for change precede commitment to change.

7. *Change fails because we neglect the transition.* Figure 12-2 illustrates the distinction between change and transition. Change is the desired new state we want the organization to move toward. Transition, on the other hand, is the process of moving from the status quo at X to the new situation. For organizations to change, we must attend to the transition process.

This process of transition always begins by letting go of some part of the past. The challenge here is that you cannot see where you are going to land.

8. *Change fails because we are not structured for change.* The leadership of any organization is faced with the challenge of balancing two fundamental tasks: (1) doing the job, and (2) getting better at doing that job. Balancing these two tasks is a challenge because they are incompatible: that is, "getting better" is in conflict with "doing" or "getting by" (see Figure 12-3). Making improvements usually requires that we stop doing something long enough to figure out how to do it better. And getting better can be very difficult for several reasons:

Figure 12-2. Transition vs. change.

Figure 12-3. The challenge to find the right balance between operations—getting by—and improvement—getting better.

**GETTING
BY**

GETTING
BETTER

- *We do not see the need for change.* With growth, each person's overall view of the organization tends to shrink. Since people see only parts of the organization, they also see only parts of problems, and it gets very hard to figure out what is really going on and how to improve things.
- *We lose a strategic sense.* As people address the problems that they see from their limited viewpoints, they may lose sight of the bigger picture and the strategic priorities.
- *We cannot get the right people together.* With the vertical and lateral spread of the organization, it becomes harder and harder to get the right people together long enough even to figure out what the problem is, let alone solve it.
- *We are too busy.* Customer demands and the push for "results" in a rapidly growing organization often leave little time for thought, planning, and development. We can easily get caught in a "too busy to think" trap.

As organizations grow and succeed, we have to recognize the need to create and sustain a special effort to "get better." Getting better will not occur naturally. In fact, if we don't make a conscious and sustained effort to get better, just the opposite will occur.

Managing Change

It is natural to want to use the normal hierarchical organization to manage change and operate improvement activities. However, trying to use the normal structure for this "getting better" effort is part of the problem and does not generally work. As shown in Figure 12-4, the normal or operational structure is de-

Figure 12-4. Differences in outlook between operational and developmental structures.

Operational Structure		Developmental Structure
Doing day-to-day operations	**FOCUS**	Improving day-to-day operations
Hierarchical	**STRUCTURE**	Collegial
Relatively repetitive	**TYPE OF WORK**	Relatively creative
Short-term, small picture	**FRAMEWORK**	Long-term, big picture
Urgent and important	**PRIORITIES**	Important, not urgent
90% – 95%	**EFFORT SPENT**	5% – 15%
Arrest the problem and treat the symptoms	**SOLUTIONS**	Uncover assumptions and find root causes

signed for the world of "doing." Getting better—developing, if you will—requires the organization to enter new territory by challenging old assumptions and creating new alternatives.

Building and sustaining a lasting improvement and development program requires that we separate the "getting better" activities from the "doing" activities and manage the improvement effort with a totally different set of structures, processes, and procedures. Since most organizations have little skill in successfully managing organizationwide change, it is helpful to have a structure and a system for designing and implementing change. This system is composed of several overlapping teams (see Figure 12-5). There are two fundamental types of teams in the system: (1) the development team, which orchestrates all other teams and sits at the center of a node, and (2) the task teams, which are created by the development team to tackle specific tasks and which share one or two members with the development team.

The Development Team and Task Teams

The development team is a permanent team that is responsible for managing the ongoing, overall change and improvement ef-

Figure 12-5. A developmental structure with one permanent development team addressing a strategic, organizationwide agenda and two temporary task teams addressing strategic problems in a subsystem.

OPERATIONAL STRUCTURE   DEVELOPMENTAL STRUCTURE

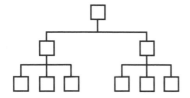
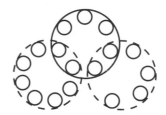

fort. It focuses on strategic issues and expands its effort by launching and supporting temporary task teams. Task teams are disbanded when they have finished their assigned tasks. The relationship between these two types of teams is like that of a space station and its set of satellites.

The development team is composed of the head of the organizational unit together with all her direct reports. In addition, at least one person who reports to each direct report should be included. By rotating this person every six months, everyone in the top three levels is exposed to the development team without making it overly large and cumbersome.

The ideal size is five to seven persons, but up to twelve is fine. If a larger team is required, consider creating a core development team of five to seven people that handles the monthly developmental activities. This core can then be expanded for activities that require more depth, such as work on the strategic design factors of the organization.

Cascading

As shown in Figure 12-5, a typical organization has one corporate development team. If the agenda is too large for that one team, it is possible to create cascaded development teams, like those shown in Figure 12-6. Thus, the overall corporate development team may launch a development team in each department.

Figure 12-6. A cascaded development team with its own task team.

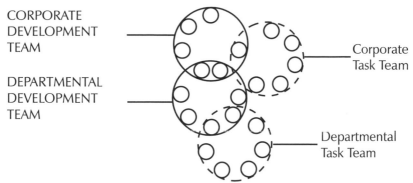

CORPORATE
DEVELOPMENT
TEAM

DEPARTMENTAL
DEVELOPMENT
TEAM

Corporate
Task Team

Departmental
Task Team

Each departmental development team has two members on the corporate development team—the department head and a direct report. Departmental development teams should also consider linking across functional lines by including members from other departments critical to their success.

How a Development System Operates

The way the development system works is fairly simple. Problems or issues of concern from any source are fed into the system (see Figure 12-7). This is the raw material that must be sorted and analyzed by the development team. Apparent problems may surface in a part of the organization that cannot define or solve them. The development team defines and prioritizes problems into real strategic problems, which it passes on to those who can solve them. And finally, the development team designs, supports, and monitors task teams to ensure results.

Remember, many problems do not get solved because they cut across organizational boundaries, and the barrier of the culture can block cross-functional problem solving. Without waiting until the whole structure and culture changes to better support strategic change, the developmental structure and system creates a mechanism for sustaining responsible change. Indirectly, it also becomes a major mechanism for changing the whole structure and culture of the organization.

Figure 12-7. The flow of problems in a developmental structure and system.

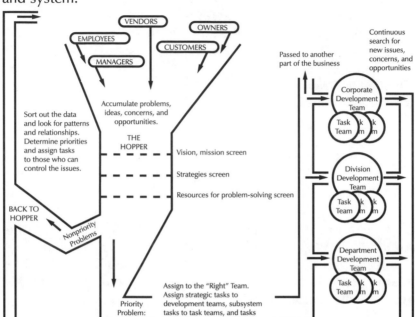

All organizations can bring to the surface more problems than they have resources for solving. Thus, the critical role of the development team is to determine which problems to solve and which not to solve. Such strategic priorities cannot be set without considering the whole system of the organization, including key external factors.

The developmental structure and system creates an efficient, interactive clearinghouse for setting overall strategic priorities based on real-time input.

The developmental structure and system nurtures the growth of responsibility. Participating in the developmental structure and system enables members to see more of the whole system of the business and to better understand and appreciate the complex interrelationships of the elements. This enables each person to make more and more decisions that take the whole into account.

It is the ongoing responsibility of each development team to constantly scan what is going on in its piece of the organization and to bring to the surface new issues to be handled by the system. In its regular sessions, the team makes sure that key problems are generated, defined, prioritized, and channeled to the appropriate level for action and that processes that are action-oriented and participative are employed to solve them. The team does this by ensuring that the right people (that is, those with enough authority, power, and expertise) are assigned to well-defined tasks and that they work to specified deadlines to produce long-term solutions.

The development team operates differently from the senior management team on the operational side of the business. The development team strives to model the desired culture of the organization. Members interact as peers, using their knowledge and experience to explore issues and seek consensus.

The most serious sin that development teams must avoid at all costs is to attack, undermine, or surprise the operational system. If this occurs, the operational system will invariably begin to discount the development team and all its work.

Results You Can Expect From a Development System

In organizations that have implemented a permanent development structure for getting better, four goals are achieved simultaneously:

1. *Organizational results.* Persistent and complex strategic problems are solved.

2. *Culture change.* The organization's sense of teamwork and participation is significantly enhanced.

3. *Professional growth.* Problem-solving sessions provide management training when participants share what they know about needs and problems in their departments. The system itself becomes a highly effective forum for meaningful manage-

ment training and increasing business literacy as accountants learn about marketing and sales learns about inventory control.

4. *Personal growth.* Responsible teams enable individuals to confront their shortcomings, gain new perspectives, and grow as human beings.

Momentum Guidelines for Development Teams

Developmental improvements generally take two to three years to achieve. Success requires 20 percent good thinking and 80 percent persistence to keep the development team meeting and active. Normally, the energy and focus for developmental activity decline significantly in about three months and are overwhelmed by operational pressures in six to twelve months.

In general, a successful development team meets monthly for at least a four- to six-hour session. Quarterly meetings are fine for reviewing changes but inadequate for fueling changes.

Successful organizational change efforts are based on redesigning the organization. This is a slow process. One way to deal with this is through armoring to protect the development process from short-term pressures and the lack of discipline to follow through. In armoring we make decisions now to support and strengthen our commitment to long-term improvement—for example, by scheduling monthly development team meetings twelve to eighteen months in advance to avoid time conflicts.

Changing the Culture

Culture is crucial, and changing it is not a widely understood process.

The culture of an organization emerges early in its history as a result of the personalities and actions of its leaders, which become institutionalized in the company's policies, procedures, systems, structure, decisions, and day-to-day actions.

In most organizations the leaders have not consciously designed the culture, but a culture emerges nevertheless. In other cases, the leaders' laissez-faire attitude allows strong individual managers to play a major role in creating the culture. The less focused and persistent the leaders' attitudes and values are, the more likely it is that different departments or divisions will have different cultures.

Culture is hard to change because it is nebulous, both a result and a cause of what is going on in the organization. Cultures are essentially self-perpetuating. However, to get substantial organizational change, you must generally change the culture. This takes time, effort, and commitment, but it can be done.

Diagnosing the Culture

If the organization has conducted a thorough diagnosis, this should yield a good starting place for understanding the current culture. An even deeper understanding of the culture and its strategic impact can be developed by looking beneath and behind a dozen recent decisions to get to the underlying attitudes, values, and beliefs that would have to be in place to arrive at such decisions. In doing so, you get a list of elements in the organization's culture. To be useful, this list must be honest. It must describe how the culture "is," not how it "should be" or how you might want it to be. Sharing this description of the culture with other employees is a good way to test its accuracy.

The next step is to evaluate how well the actual culture supports the strategic plan. Explore what elements of the culture support the plan and which are barriers. Consider adding any missing elements.

Specifying the Culture Change

As the diagnosis progresses, it becomes possible to specify the desired culture change. This should not be a laundry list of all good things that could possibly be in the culture. It should focus on the key areas to add or change in order to better support strategic change. Here is a sample culture statement that focuses on teamwork and results:

We at XYZ Corporation agree to work aggressively this
year to change our culture. In each meeting and interaction with our fellow team members, we will work to
be:

- More aggressive in making decisions and
  taking actions to maintain our results orientation.
- More responsive and responsible to our fellow team members. We will attempt to help
  each other to identify and solve problems
  and will follow through on assignments
  we've accepted and commitments we've
  made.
- More open and honest in our communication, realizing that only in this way will we
  be able to efficiently address and solve the
  tough issues at XYZ Corporation.
- More respectful of the time of others by
  coming on time to all meetings and devot-
  ing full time at these meetings to the task at
  hand.
- More respectful of the opinions, perspectives, and insights of others. We realize that
  every problem has many different perspectives to it, and we also know that one or
  more of our teammates at XYZ Corporation
  may have a perspective we don't have.
  Therefore, we will work hard to identify different perspectives on our problems. We
  will listen carefully to the opinions and perspectives of our teammates so we can learn
  from them and create better solutions at
  XYZ Corporation.

Taking Actual Steps

The Role of the Leader

The first step in installing your desired culture is for the
company president to meet in small groups with all employees.

The president announces the desired culture change, explains why it is strategically important to the company's success, and answers questions.

Culture is not created by signs, slogans, memos, or motivational speeches. Employees know that what the leader does is more important than what he says. Leaders who want to communicate learn to walk their talk. Since the culture is created by the behavior of the leaders, it can only be changed when the behavior of the leaders changes.

To help you keep on track, periodically ask those you lead to tell you how well your personal behavior is supporting the desired culture change. Also, ask for specific examples of how your personal behavior does and does not support the desired culture.

Solving Problems

The single most powerful way to change an organization's culture is by solving problems with a process that uses the desired culture change. The problems selected must be of real concern. Thus, if there is poor interdepartmental teamwork and the desired culture encourages such teamwork, choose a significant problem between two departments and solve it by having department members work together as one team to solve it.

The result of such task teams is twofold. First, they solve problems that are of concern. Second, they do it using the new culture, for example, through mutual respect, openness, and teamwork. This changes the culture by demonstrating the value of the new culture—it helped solve the problem.

Strategic Alignment With the Culture

The organization's strategic alignment must ensure that the structure, staffing, systems, allocation of resources, and sanctions support the culture. Organizational alignment occurs when these five strategic factors support the culture. It takes several years to systematically change and align these five elements. When this alignment occurs, the new culture is on its way to being institutionalized.

Cultural Communications

The important items in the culture change must be communicated continually in announcements and memos (the least effective methods), in rituals, ceremonies, stories, logos, symbols, and training. These last six methods are more concrete and effective.

The Cultural Review

If you are really serious about installing and maintaining a desired culture change, you can assemble a task force to assess progress on culture change every three to six months. This is most easily done by selecting a handful of major decisions, changes, and any crisis that the organization responded to during the period being reviewed. These are now held up against the statement of desired culture change to see if, in fact, the culture influenced the responses.

It is also possible to simply make a list of the desired culture items and have a group rate how strongly and consistently they believe the items are being pursued on a scale from one to ten. Redoing this rating every three to four months gives you a baseline sense of whether progress is being made.

Ensuring Responsible Change

Responsible change efforts demand three things from everyone involved in the improvement activities.

1. *Responsibility.* The problems we are trying to solve are everyone's problems. They do not belong to Jane or Harry; they are ours. We helped to identify them, and we are responsible for seeing that they are resolved. The problems were relatively easy to identify but will not be easy to resolve. Everyone must be willing to carry his or her share of the load.

2. *Patience.* Successful organizational change efforts are a slow process. There are no quick fixes that produce deep change.

Sustainable improvements take two to three years but result in dramatically more healthy and exciting organizations. With the excitement and energy created in the initial phases of an organizational improvement program, the normal tendency is to try to do too much too soon. This is usually manifested by the launching of too many task teams (more than three). When this happens, people quickly become overinvolved and end up having too little time for their regular duties. People should devote about 90 to 95 percent of their time to doing their jobs and only 5 to 10 percent of their time to these improvement activities.

3. *Discipline.* The discipline of change refers to the regularity with which change is pursued as well as the emerging skills that are developed through devotion to change. Individuals and organizations that pursue their goals with discipline outperform brilliant strategies and elegant methods.[6]

Authenticity combines with discipline to produce remarkable results. Authenticity means that you do what you say and say what you do—there are no cover-ups. It captures people's hearts and commitment.

What Next

Most of us find more fun, energy, and interest in selecting which changes to make than in the long-term follow-up, discipline, and perseverance it takes to implement change. Like dieting, it's easier to choose the next diet than it is to lose the weight.

For this reason, the authors conduct a basic boot camp on understanding organizations and how they change. More important, we orchestrate ongoing support groups for CEOs and internal change agents to develop the knowledge, skill, and discipline to create responsible companies.

Notes

1. See Ken Meyers and Ron Ash Kenas, "Results Driven Quality Now," *Management Review*, March 1993, and Jay Matthews and Peter Katel, "The Cost

of Quality Faced With Hard Times—Business Sours on TQM," *Newsweek,*
Sept. 7, 1992.
2. "Reengineering—The Hot New Management Tool," *Fortune,* Aug. 23, 1993.
3. "The Baldrige's Other Award," *Business Week,* March 10, 1997.
4. The Cycle of Change is a combination of the ideas of Frederick Hudson in
The Adult Years (San Francisco: Jossey-Bass, 1991), Marv Weissbord in *Future
Search* (San Francisco: Berrett-Koehler, 1995), and Ichak Adizes in *Corporate
Life Cycles* (Englewood Cliffs, N.J.: Prentice Hall, 1988).
5. Frederick Hudson, *The Adult Years.*
6. James Collins and Jerry Porras, *Built to Last: Successful Habits of Visionary
Companies* (New York: Harper Business, 1994).

Index

The letter *f* after a number indicates that the information is contained in a figure.